Praise for
Be True to Yourself

"*Be True to Yourself* is full of great advice and wisdom. Each day you can read something that will make that day just a little bit brighter."

—Kimberly Kirberger, coauthor of *Chicken Soup for the Teenage Soul*, author of the Teen Love series

"Hardly a day goes by when I don't wonder how I will help my daughter keep her soul intact as she grows up. Straightforward and truthful, Amanda Ford's book may be one of the answers."

—Jennifer Louden, author of *The Woman's Comfort Book* and *The Comfort Queen's Guide to Life*

BE
TRUE
TO
YOURSELF

BE
TRUE
TO
YOURSELF

Daily Affirmations
and Awesome Advice
for Teen Girls

AMANDA FORD

Conari
Press

CORAL GABLES

Cover, Layout & Design: Morgane Leoni

For permission requests, please contact the publisher at:
Mango Publishing Group
2850 S Douglas Road, 2nd Floor
Coral Gables, FL 33134 USA
info@mangopublishinggroup.com

For special orders, quantity sales, course adoptions and corporate sales, please
email the publisher at sales@mango.bz. For trade and wholesale sales, please
contact Ingram Publisher Services at customer.service@ingramcontent.com or
+1.800.509.4887.

Be True to Yourself: Daily Affirmations and Awesome Advice for Teen Girls

Library of Congress Cataloging-in-Publication number: pending
ISBN: (print) 978-1-64250-451-4, (ebook) 978-1-64250-452-1
BISAC category code: YAN051200, YOUNG ADULT NONFICTION / Social
Topics / Self-Esteem & Self-Reliance

Printed in the United States of America

For every girl who
has ever wondered:

Do I belong?
(You do.)

Am I okay?
(You are.)

Will I get through this?
(You will.)

Preface

Twenty years ago, I was twenty years old and I got the idea to write a book for teenage girls filled with all the perspective and advice I might offer to a younger sister, the words and guidance I wished I'd had myself. The following year, the first edition of *Be True to Yourself* was published.

The book was well-received. I still have a stack of handwritten letters that arrived to me in the mail (yep, snailmail!) from girls telling me how the book had touched and inspired them.

A lot has changed in twenty years, and although adolescence is long behind me, my concern and affection for girls of this age remains. From family ties to friendship connections, I am fortunate to have many tween and teen girls in my life. It is with these enthusiastic, spirited, stubborn, talented, smart, and utterly delightful girls in mind that I revised *Be True to Yourself* for this second edition you now hold in your hands.

Our future depends on the well-being and abilities of our young people. It is essential that our kids—girls and boys—emerge from their teenage years with their hearts strong, their intellects sharp, and their imaginations wild and intact. My hope is that this book serves as a small resource to help with that goal.

Introduction

I remember vividly the day my high school art teacher told us that she didn't care too much about how well we did in her class. "What I do care about," she said, "is that maybe someday when you are an adult, you will think of this class and you will say to yourself, 'I remember I enjoyed making art,' and you will pick up a brush or a pencil and you will create something again." Her statement impacted me with its clear message that I didn't need to be moving on a direct and certain path. Her statement told me that I could pick up where I left off, that I could—and would—be discovering and rediscovering myself for years and decades to come.

My art teacher understood her job as planting seeds of possibility in our minds and hearts.

That's exactly how I see this book: As little seeds of possibility that will bloom when they are needed. It is full of practical advice, pep talks, and poetic inspiration to help you in the journey of discovering and being true to yourself.

Being true to yourself is not easy. It might mean going against the beliefs and actions of your peers. It might mean disappointing somebody you love. You might wonder, "Who am I anyway?" Sometimes you won't know what to do. Sometimes you will do something that will turn out to be the wrong thing and you will feel very bad about it, but that's okay, because getting off course is an unavoidable part of getting to know yourself.

I hope this book will serve as a guidepost along the way, encouraging your imagination, nourishing your heart, and fortifying your sense of self-worth. I hope this book will be an antidote to all that is superficial, harsh, and fleeting, an antidote to all the things that might rob you of knowing your innate magnificence.

This book is organized in short essays, one to read for every day of the year. You can read it in order day by day, from cover to cover in one sitting, or flip through and read randomly as you feel called. Some ideas will resonate for you, some will not. Take what works for you and leave the rest. Words that don't make sense at first might someday become the very thing you need to hear.

The fact that you are reading this book tells me that you are a special soul, a deeper thinker, and a curious seeker. I am grateful and honored to be connected to you through the shared experience of these pages.

Let's dive in...

DAY 1: **FINGERPRINT**

 Hello!

You are here, alive, eyes open. Your eyes are the window to your soul, and did you know that the swirls and whirls inside your iris pools are unique to you?

Look in the mirror. Look at the colorful part of your eyes. These are your irises. The subtle lines, dots, and variations of color you see inside those irises are extraordinary, because those patterns only exist inside of you.

Never before did a person have those patterns in their eyes. Never again will those patterns be recreated.

Jeepers creepers, your peepers prove it! And so do your tongue and your fingerprint and your toe-print and your lip-print and your tongue and even your teeth: There is nobody like you.

DAY 2: **UNIQUELY YOU**

 There is nobody like you. This is an essential truth that you must accept deep in your heart.

No one on earth can do what you do in quite the way that you do it. You have your own spin, your own flair, your very own special sauce.

It is of utmost importance that you forever honor the unique and rare person that you are. If you do not, the world will miss out on all the special surprises you have to offer.

Over the course of this book, I hope you will come to see and appreciate yourself even more clearly, but for today, just let it sink in: There is nobody like you.

DAY 3: **DO + BE**

 What do you want to do, dear girl? Who do you want to be?

These are the questions worth contemplating forever into eternity. These are essential questions of life, and your answers will make your life your own.

Whether you know it yet or not, your life is yours to create. Even as your parents make the rules. Even as you work to fit in with your friends. Even as school consumes your time.

Your life is yours to create even inside these seemingly confining boxes.

How will you make it your own? What will you discover about yourself? Who will you choose to be? Where will you find belonging and meaning? What will you do with your unique life?

DAY 4: **SCAVENGER HUNT**

 Who am I? Who do I want to be? Where do I belong? What do I want to do?

Maybe you can answer these questions easily. Maybe you cannot. Or maybe you can, but your current answers will change next week, next year, or next decade.

Being true to yourself is like a lifelong scavenger hunt. You use your curiosity, your heart, your intellect, your intuition, and your imagination to decipher clues along the way. One clue leads to the next, which leads to the next, which leads to the next...

Eventually you reach the greatest reward of all: your true self.

What makes you excited? What are you good at? Who is kind to you? Who makes you laugh? Where do you feel at home?

Your answers to these questions are some of the clues that point you in the right direction. If you keep your eyes open and your mind bright, you will uncover many more clues throughout this book, as well as scattered about in the world as you go about your daily life.

DAY 5: **YOUR TWO LIVES**

 Do you know that you live two lives: An outer life and an inner life?

Your outer life consists of all the things that take place in the material world, like your food, your clothes, your activities, and your own experiences. Your inner life consists of all the varied thoughts, feelings, and sensations that happen inside your mind, heart, and body.

Imagine you and a friend have an adventure together. You can tell the story of your adventure from the perspective of your outer world or your inner world.

The outer world version tells the facts: "We went berry picking and I saw a snake and I was so scared that I jumped back so fast and the berries from my basket dumped all over me. Turns out it wasn't even a snake; it was a rope!"

The inner world version tells how you felt: "I felt happy, with my mouth watering at the smell of ripe berries, but when I saw the snake, I felt terrified and then a little embarrassed when we realized it was a rope, but we laughed so hard about it that I felt happy again."

Can you notice the difference between your outer life and your inner life today?

DAY 6: **WHERE THE MAGIC HAPPENS**

 I'm going to let you in on a secret: Many people believe that your outer world is the most important thing about your life, but it is actually your inner world where the magic of your life takes place.

Somebody can have a perfect outer life with lots of friends, great clothes, a nice house, and school awards, but still feel unhappy, anxious, bored, and dissatisfied inside themselves. It is possible and even common for one's outer and inner lives to be mismatched.

There is so much in your outer world beyond your control, and outer world success is often determined by the sheer randomness of luck.

Your inner world, however, is entirely within your hands to cultivate, nurture, and grow.

DAY 7: **RESILIENCE**

Having a steady and deep inner world will make the unexpected challenges that appear in your outer world easier to navigate.

A strong inner world makes you resilient. It means you have resources inside yourself to cope when friends leave you out, when you struggle to understand the lesson in a class, when you have a fight with your parents, when your crush breaks your heart, when get you sick, when a pet dies, or when any other hard thing happens in your outer world.

A strong inner life doesn't mean that hard things won't hurt. It just means that you will survive, thrive, and move past them.

Understanding even a little bit of your inner world will help you tremendously during your teenage years and beyond. The simple fact that you even know that these two enmeshed aspects of your life exist is powerful knowledge.

Today, consider what the word *resilience* means to you. What do you do to help yourself bounce back from difficult events? Your answers to these questions will give you clues about your own inner life.

DAY 8: **WORTHY**

 You do not need to be perfect or pretty. Not at all. You do not need to be smart or talented or adored. You do not need to accomplish anything remarkable. You do not need to win an award.

You simply need to be here. Being here is enough. Being you, as you are, is enough.

Your worth does not have to be proven or earned. Your worth is inherent.

You are worthy because you are here. And that is the truth. Even if you don't know it.

No matter what happens to you in this life, no matter what challenges you face, no matter what mistakes you make, you cannot escape or erase your worth.

You are worthy. Even if you don't believe it.

And if you forget it, just come back and reread this page and trust that it is true.

DAY 9: **TAKE A LITTLE TIME**

 Take a little time every day to look up and out as far as your eyes can see.

Take a little time every day to notice that you are alive. Can you feel the way your body fills and relaxes with each breath? Can you sense your heartbeat?

Take time every day to check in with yourself. How are you? What do you need to lift up your spirit?

Take a little time every day to be delighted by something, anything. Pause when it happens. Take note.

Take a little time every day, just one minute even, to do absolutely nothing. Can you feel the weight of gravity in your bones? Can you relax your muscles? Can you sense space in your joints?

Take a little time every day.

DAY 10: **BEAUTIFUL**

 You are beautiful in the same way that the moon is beautiful.

Eternally beautiful.

Beautiful without question.

DAY 11: **DISCOVER + CHOOSE**

 To be true to yourself requires you to do two things: *Discover* and *choose*.

You must discover your true self, dig below the surface and search past the obvious, go deeper and higher, beyond identity labels like *smart, funny, athletic.* Who are you at your core? Who are you in your soul?

You must also choose. Whenever and wherever there is a choice to be made, you get to make it. You decide how you conduct yourself, how you treat others, how you let others treat you, how you spend your time, and what thoughts you allow to consume your mind. You choose your friends, your clothes, and your hobbies. You choose—each and every day—how loyal you will be to your soul.

Being true to yourself is about learning to ride the tide *and* learning to steer the ship.

DAY 12: **PAY ATTENTION**

Pay attention! might sound like an annoying command from your parents when they are scolding you or by your teachers when they are lecturing the class.

Paying attention, however, is perhaps one of the greatest skills you can cultivate to get to know yourself, strengthen your inner world, and enrich your experience of your outer world.

Paying attention fosters your curiosity, hones your intuition, and inspires your creativity.

Paying attention is a skill we must practice. We must decide to put down distractions and take note. Paying attention is a deliberate choice.

There will be many times throughout this book when I will encourage you to "pay attention" and "notice." These words are not orders to you, but rather invitations for you to wake up both to the world around you and to your life.

DAY 13: **WRITING YOURSELF**

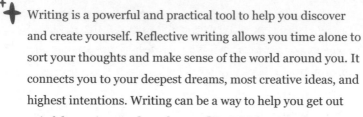 Writing is a powerful and practical tool to help you discover and create yourself. Reflective writing allows you time alone to sort your thoughts and make sense of the world around you. It connects you to your deepest dreams, most creative ideas, and highest intentions. Writing can be a way to help you get out painful emotions and resolve conflict. Writing can also connect you to your spiritual source.

Throughout this book, you will find writing prompts to inspire your imagination and encourage your critical thinking. Do these writings in a journal or on sheets of paper, but definitely do them by hand. Writing by hand engages your brain in a way that typing on a computer does not.

Here's your first writing prompt: The words you use to describe yourself inside your own mind impact your self-image and hold tremendous power in shaping the way your life unfolds. What are the words you use to describe yourself? Are there any words you wish were not on this list? Are there any words that you wish were on this list? Write whatever thoughts come to mind. There are no wrong answers.

DAY 14: **JOURNAL**

A journal is a document of your life, of the things you did and how you felt about those things. It can include writing, doodling, painting, or collage. It is a private place where you express yourself without filters or fear of what others might think.

A journal is not a place where you need to get things perfect. Let your journal be a place where you can be free. "Mistakes" are just part of the process. You don't have to rip out pages and start over. You can write words on top of words, draw cats in the margins, cross everything out with straight lines, or add color.

A journal is your place to explore ideas and get to know yourself better.

Do you have a journal? If not, you might consider getting one. It doesn't have to be a fancy thing. It can be a simple spiral notebook. It's not what the journal looks like, but rather the journey that matters.

DAY 15: **WRITING FREELY**

 For many of the writing prompts in this book, I will encourage you to write freely. Unlike an essay for school, when writing freely, it is better if you don't think too hard about what you put on the page.

Writing freely lets your thoughts spill out without you editing or even trying to make sense of them. When writing freely, keep your pen moving as much as possible and don't correct yourself along the way. Nobody's going to read what you write, and you can rip the paper into a million pieces as soon as you're done if you want.

The purpose of writing freely is to get past your surface thoughts and automatic reactions. During the process, you might discover something new about yourself or come up with a solution to a problem you've been having.

A good guideline is to allow three to ten minutes for writing freely.

Give it a try right now by writing freely about the following questions: What is the hardest thing you've ever had to do? What made it so hard? How did you get through it? Did you have help along the way? Did you learn anything about yourself in the end?

DAY 16: **WRITING YOUR INNER LIFE + OUTER LIFE**

 What do you want to do? Who do you want to be? Remember these questions from several days back?

What do you want to do? is a question about your outer life: things like the classes you take, the grades you earn, the clothes you wear, how you keep your bedroom, and the activities you participate in.

Who do you want to be? is a question about your inner life. Things like your character traits, your imagination, and your spiritual perspective.

Write the answers to the questions *what do you want to do?* and *who do you want to be?* Write for five minutes without picking up your pen from the page. Let your thoughts flow without critique. There are no wrong answers. Write in a journal, on a random piece of paper, or in the margins of this very page.

DAY 17: **NOT A MACHINE**

 You are not a machine.

You are not a computer.

You are not an app.

You are a human, made of flesh.

You are full of unexpected arrivals, surprise parties, and U-turns.

And that, dear girl, is exactly what makes you so magnificent.

DAY 18: **CHEESE**

 I've got good news and bad news. Which do you want first?

The bad news?

Okay. Here goes...

Not everyone is going to like you. Some people will really, *really* dislike you, no matter what. The good news, however, is that if somebody doesn't like you, it actually has nothing to do with you.

Consider this in terms of food. Some people love cheese. Some feel so-so about cheese. Others DO NOT LIKE cheese. All these opinions have nothing to do with cheese and everything to do with the person's preferences and worldview. Maybe it's the physiology of their unique taste buds. Maybe they are vegan or are lactose intolerant.

It's not about the cheese, per se. The cheese is just cheese doing its cheesy thing. Many people think cheese is the most delicious creation in the history of food.

So there's no reason for the cheese to feel bad about itself.

Same goes for you.

DAY 19: **PIVOTAL MOMENT**

 Cheryl's two closest friends did not like each other. They were very different girls. One wanted to do well in school and followed rules. The other one didn't care about school and broke rules often.

For many years she had been friends with both of them, and they each represented a side of her. Cheryl wanted to do well in school

AMANDA FORD

and liked to please her parents, but she also had a wild side and liked exploring boundaries.

As she got older, the divide between her two friends grew. School became more demanding while, at the same time, the risks being taken had higher stakes. It became clear to Cheryl that she could not travel both paths. She had to choose the kind of girl she wanted to be and the kind of life she wanted to create.

It is true that you can build a life that is unique and you don't need to fit yourself into a tightly defined box, but it is also true that sometimes you will encounter a fork in the road and you will have to make a hard and clear choice about where you will go and who you will be.

DAY 20: **THE ONLY ONE**

 There will be times in your life when you are the only one.

Maybe you are the only one with your skin color in the room or the only one speaking up to the bully. Maybe you'll be the only one whose mother died or the only one with a very particular struggle.

There are times in life that we have to stand alone. Life gives us our own unique set of challenges, and it is up to us to sort through them, make sense of them, and keep going despite them.

You might be the only one in the room, but you are not the only one who has ever had to stand at one time or another. You are part of a lineage of brave women who stood up, stood out, spoke up, and kept believing in themselves, even when they seemed not to fit in.

DAY 21: **TO QUOTE ELEANOR ROOSEVELT**

 "No one can make you feel inferior without your consent."

This is a quote from Eleanor Roosevelt who was the First Lady of the United States from 1933 to 1945. She was a controversial figure because she was outspoken and active in promoting human rights throughout the world. At the time it wasn't customary for a wife of a president to speak out with such conviction. On some occasions, she even publicly disagreed with the policies that her husband put into place.

What does Eleanor Roosevelt's quote from above mean to you? Are there ways in which you consent to feeling inferior? How might you change this? Write freely about how you interpret her words. There is no right or wrong answer.

DAY 22: **MIRACULOUS YOU**

 Consider this: The human being that you are today started as a cluster of cells.

Inside your mother, you grew day by day, without school assignments or tests to pass. You didn't have anybody watching over you to make sure you were getting things done at the proper time and in the proper way.

Your body just grew, on its own, cell by cell, day by day. Your body knew what to do. It knew how to form itself. It knew how to come into the world. Ta-da! You arrived!

Seeds become sprouts and then trees. You became a baby and then a toddler and now a teenager.

Isn't that a glorious miraculous magic trick?

AMANDA FORD

DAY 23: **SPIRITUAL**

Your spirituality will be an essential tool to help you through all the challenging emotions and adversity that you will experience in life.

Spirituality is a collection of the beliefs, experiences, and practices that shape the way you understand the universe, humanity, and your specific role in it all.

Spirituality is often associated with religion, but you can have a spiritual perspective without religion. Philosophy, mythology, certain sciences, and the arts are other fields of study that can help inform your spiritual perspective.

Spirituality explores some of life's most complex questions: What is the meaning of life? What is on the edge of the universe? What happens to a person when they die? Is there a dimension beyond the physical realm? Who am I? What is my responsibility to others?

Here's a writing prompt to encourage your spiritual thinking: What does your soul know that your mind forgets sometimes?

DAY 24: **FINE**

Sometimes you say, "I'm fine," even when you are not, because it's just too much to say how or where it hurts.

You are not alone. That girl across the room, she does that too. So does that guy who seems to have it all.

"I'm fine," you say, even when you are not.

Sometimes you are not fine, and in this you are not alone.

It's okay to not feel fine and it's okay if you pretend that you do.

Someday the pain will go away. Someday it might even make sense.

Someday, because you know this pain, you will be able to help somebody else when they say, "I'm fine," but you can see in their eyes that they are not.

Someday you will see that this very pain was the thing that made your heart so big, so capable of feeling so much.

DAY 25: **DO YOUR BEST WITH WHAT YOU'VE GOT**

 Always do your best. Take care in your work. Give it your all.

In anything you must do and in everything you choose to do, do your best with what you've got.

This means doing the best you can in this moment, given your circumstances and the resources available to you.

Some days, you will be energetic and focused, and your best effort will look like a masterpiece. Other days, you will be low and overwhelmed and your best effort will look like a scribble.

Cumulatively, however, your best effort in all things added up over time will lead you to a successful and meaningful life.

DAY 26: **IMPERFECT ACTION**

 Doing your best with what you've got does not actually mean performing perfectly.

Sometimes we believe that giving our all to something means doing it in a way that is exactly *correct*. When we aim for

AMANDA FORD

perfect, however, we often become paralyzed, unable to do much of anything at all. Moving forward with imperfect action is much better than staying stuck while waiting for the perfect moment to act.

Imperfect action means taking a step even though you are scared or believe you are unprepared. Imperfect action is moving forward without overthinking or comparing your journey to the journey of somebody else. When you take imperfect action, you know that mistakes are an unavoidable part of the process, not signs that there is something wrong with you.

DAY 27: IMPERFECT ACTION + PROPER MINDSET = PROGRESS

I call this the magical life equation. No matter what it is you want to achieve, when you pair imperfect action with a proper mindset, you make progress in life.

When you have a proper mindset you are open, curious, flexible, and lighthearted. You do not overindulge your fear and are not critical of yourself or others. Keeping a proper mindset means keeping faith that life is full of options, even if you cannot see them right now.

Progress is any forward movement, no matter how small, toward your goal. Keep in mind that true progress does not exploit Mother Earth, other human beings, or animals for the sake of one's own ego, celebrity, or pocketbook.

Whether you want to make more friends, improve your grades in school, get better at an activity you love, or develop a new skill, if you take imperfect action while keeping a proper mindset, you'll make progress.

DAY 28: **DIRECT YOUR ATTENTION**

 At any given moment you can direct your attention wherever you'd like.

Right now, notice your right foot. Look at it. What do you see? A shoe? A sock? Can you wiggle your toes? Do you have any sensations in your foot?

Next bring your attention to your breath. Can you feel its rise and fall? Can you feel the air move in and out through your nose?

Then look as far into the distance as you can. What do you see there? Focus your attention there and breathe for several moments before reading any more of this page.

In the same way that you just moved your attention from one thing to another, you can also move your attention away from certain thoughts and toward others. If you find yourself thinking negative or unhelpful thoughts, can you move your attention to a more positive and helpful thought? Give it a try.

DAY 29: **WRITING BEAUTY**

 There are two sayings, "Beauty is only skin-deep" and "It's what's on the inside that counts."

What do these sayings mean to you? Do these ideas resonate as true for you? How do these ideas show up in your own life? How can you show what's inside of you on the outside of you? What does the word *beauty* mean to you? When do you feel beautiful?

Write freely the answers to these questions and any other thoughts they inspire for you.

DAY 30: **HEALTHY SOUL**

 It is a common belief that caring for your mind, body, and soul will give you a balanced life. You keep your mind healthy through intellectual stimulation. You keep your body healthy through good nutrition and regular movement.

But how do you keep your soul healthy?

Your soul is the part inside of you that feels amazed by the sunrise, cries during sad movies, and is touched by the sound of beautiful music. It's the part of you that gets excited about living, about waking up on a sunny morning, and about laughing really hard with your friends.

Today, pay attention to your soul. How is your soul doing? What is it saying? What signals is it sending you? What is it telling you to do? Your soul is your highest self, and simply learning to listen when it guides you is how you will keep your soul healthy.

DAY 31: **YOU ARE NATURE**

 Spending time in nature is some of the best medicine for your mind and soul. Simply noticing the natural world around you can wake you up, inspire your imagination, and help you feel less stressed, less bored, and less alone.

This is because you *are* nature. Human beings have created elaborate systems and technologies in attempts to tame the wild unpredictability of nature. We live inside buildings that keep the elements out. We eat food that comes from factories. We turn on lights to stay awake.

None of these inventions change the fact that you are made of the exact same stuff that makes up the ocean, the mountains, the flowers, the butterflies, the elephants.

Notice the natural world around you today. What do you see? It surrounds you even if you live in a dense urban area. Your observations of the natural world can be as simple as noticing the change of light throughout the day, looking at the sky, feeling the air on your skin, seeing where bits of green spring to life in sidewalk cracks and between buildings, or paying attention to the indoor plants you encounter.

DAY 32: **WAG**

 What delights you, what thrills you, what excites you?

What makes you wiggle and squeal?

Have you ever seen a dog wag her tail so enthusiastically that her whole body gets in on the action?

What makes you happy like that?

DAY 33: **NOTICE THE DETAILS OF THE PEOPLE YOU LOVE**

 How many details about the people you love can you describe? Not just big, broad brushstrokes, but the specific nuances and subtleties.

Start noticing the details about the people you love. What side of their mouth does their smile start on? What does their body language look like when they are mad? How do they sit? Do they typically cross one leg over the other? Which leg?

Pay attention. What is it that you love about them? What do they do that makes you laugh, smile, feel delighted to be in their presence? Be as specific and detail oriented as you can in your observation.

DAY 34: **EMOTIONAL**

 These years of your life will be full of wild and raw emotion.

This is one of the best parts about being a teenager. Everything that is good is amazing, vibrant, and energized, buzzing, brimming, overflowing with enthusiasm and wonder.

This also one of the worst parts about being a teenager. Everything that is bad is terrible, heavy, and dismal and seems certain to never end.

This is not just because you are moody or dramatic. It's a very real phenomenon caused by the fact that the part of your brain responsible for helping you regulate emotion is not fully yet linked up with the part of your brain responsible for creating those emotions. Your brain is still growing and will continue to do so well into your twenties.

The lesson? Savor the good times in your life. They will never again be quite as potent as they are now. Develop skills to navigate the hard times, and trust that they will also lose their sharpness as you age.

DAY 35: **EMOTIONS**

 Emotions are a huge part of the human experience and an even bigger part of the teenage experience.

During this time of your life, you might find that your emotions overwhelm you at times. This is not a sign that you are moody or difficult or that something is wrong with you.

There is a biological reason why emotions hit you a lot harder during this time of your life than they will in fifteen years from now. It's because as a teen, the part of your brain devoted to controlling your emotions is not yet fully developed and won't be until your mid to late twenties.

Over the course of this book, we will explore a lot about emotions. For today, simply notice how many different emotions you feel. Can you name them as they arise?

DAY 36: **WORDS FOR SAD**

 Most of us know the words sad and depressed, but there are many other words to describe this type of emotional state. Below is a list for you to reference. Use it whenever you find yourself feeling down, but don't have the words to say exactly why. Sometimes finding the right words can help you understand and manage your feelings so that they don't overwhelm you.

Disappointed. Blue. Confused. Somber. Jealous. Numb. Blah. Mopey. Sorry. Bored. Down. Sensitive. Detached. Brokenhearted. Grief-stricken. Dejected. Beat. Discouraged. Nostalgic. Pessimistic. Sorrowful. Distressed. Gloomy. Low. Upset. Heavy-hearted. Out of sorts. Troubled. Weepy. Pensive.

Somber. Melancholy. Aloof. Helpless. Lonely. Skeptical. Sleepy. Indifferent. Tender. Longing. Wistful. Remorseful.

Can you think of other words for *sad* not on this list?

DAY 37: **WRITING SAD**

 Nobody likes to feel sad. It is never a pleasant experience.

Once you make it through, however, you might find that the sadness has left a gift in its place. Sadness can crack you open, take you to the depths of your soul, and lead you toward a truer version of yourself. Sadness can help you be more compassionate toward others when they are suffering, because you know for yourself what it feels like. It can also make you more grateful for the good things in your life.

Write about a sad time from your past. How did you get through it? Did you learn anything from the sadness? What advice would you give to somebody going through a similar situation?

DAY 38: **WORDS FOR HAPPY**

 Cheerful. Thankful. Amused. Amazed. Calm. Eager. Curious. Content. Radiant. Good-humored. Confident. Relieved. Optimistic. Expansive. Vibrant. Awake. Beaming. Friendly. Thrilled. Lighthearted. Delighted. Excited. Safe. Proud. Alert. Spellbound. Relaxed. Inspired. Friendly. Glad. Expansive. Free. Secure. Blissful. Lively. Captivated. Playful. Tickled. Upbeat. Lucky. Optimistic. Loving. Joyful. Awestruck.

Can you think of other words for *happy* not on this list?

DAY 39: **WRITING HAPPY**

 Write a poem about being happy. Start each line of the poem with the phrase, "I'm happy…"

Here's mine to give you an example:

I'm happy when I drink bubbly water with lime. I'm happy when I can write a really good rhyme.

I'm happy when the sun shines, but it's not too hot. I'm happy when I'm riding my bike. My bike's name is Dot.

I'm happy when I wake up early. I'm happy when my hair gets curly.

I'm happy for no good reason at all and I'm happy for every good reason. That's all.

DAY 40: **WORDS FOR MAD**

 Angry. Irritated. Stubborn. Defiant. Provoked. Frustrated. Furious. Impatient. Edgy. Fidgety. Aggravated. Cold. Bitter. Raging. Irked. Feisty. Embarrassed. Repelled. Resentful. Irate. Exasperated. Fuming. Blazing. Livid. Indignant. Hostile. Hot. Uptight. Mean. Contemptuous.

Can you think of other words for *mad* not on this list?

DAY 41: **WRITING MAD**

 The next time you are mad, write it out. Write all your feelings and thoughts without censoring yourself. Write until you feel the heat of your anger begin to cool.

When you have let it all out and have nothing more to write, rip the page into the tiniest pieces possible as a symbolic gesture of moving through your anger.

Invite new feelings to enter your mind and heart.

DAY 42: **WORDS FOR SCARED**

 Afraid. Worried. Frightened. Uneasy. Nervous. Anxious. Excited. Alarmed. Cautious. Panicky. Frantic. Terrified. Agitated. Unsteady. Shaky. Jumpy. Shocked. Frenetic. Frozen. Tentative. Fearful.

Can you think of other words for *scared* not on this list?

DAY 43: **WRITING SCARED**

 Bring to mind some of your fears.

Then write for ten minutes about facing your fears. What does the idea "face your fears" mean to you? What would have to do in order to face your fears? How likely is it that most of your fears will actually happen? Are some of your fears irrational fears? How might your life be different if you faced your fears?

Don't think too hard about what you write. Let your pen lead the way. Don't edit yourself. The purpose is not to get a right answer, but simply to explore ideas in hopes of getting to know yourself.

DAY 44: **WORDS FOR EMBARRASSED**

 Ashamed. Guilty. Humiliated. Humbled. Cut down. Self-conscious. Awkward. Uneasy. Red-faced. Shy. Flustered. Mortified. Crushed. Sheepish.

Can you think of other words for *embarrassed* not on this list?

DAY 45: **WRITING EMBARRASSED**

 Write down something you feel embarrassed about.

Immediately following the statement about your embarrassment, write "...but I accept myself anyway."

Repeat this for as many embarrassments as you'd like.

For example:

"I feel embarrassed that I kept messing up when I had to read out loud in English class, but I accept myself anyway."

"I feel embarrassed that my boobs are bigger than all my friends', but I accept myself anyway."

"I feel embarrassed about my family, but I accept myself anyway."

"I feel embarrassed that I don't have anybody to sit with at lunchtime, but I accept myself anyway."

DAY 46: **WRITE FIRST, ACT SECOND**

 Whenever you find yourself feeling very angry, depressed, stuck, uncertain, or overwhelmed, get out a piece of paper and write before you take any action.

Write about your feelings. Write about what you are scared might happen. Write about what you hope will happen.

Writing can help calm you, assist in focusing you, and help you get clear about what is the best action for you to take next.

Write first. Act second.

DAY 47: **UP + DOWN**

 If you are happy right now, I have something to tell you that might make you sad. If you are sad right now, I have something to tell you that might make you happy.

That something is this: the feeling you have in this moment will end.

No feeling lasts forever. A state of mind does not persist without change. Sometimes certain feelings are stronger and last longer, but no single feeling will be your permanent condition.

The goal is not to wish for eternal happiness or to avoid sadness at all costs. Instead the goal is to trust the ups and downs, to have faith in the flow.

You will go up. You will come down. You will go up. Down. Up again.

That's just what feelings do.

DAY 48: **LETTING GO**

 When I was fifteen, my first love broke up with me because of a lie some girl told about me. He believed her.

I tried everything to get him back. I literally even begged him while choking through snotty, slobbery sobs. It did not work.

I was tormented by grief. At night, I cried and stared at the ceiling and wished for all sorts of terrible things to happen to that girl.

One night, I realized that hating her and hoping for my ex to return was not helping. Something needed to change, and I understood that the only thing within my power to change was me.

I took my attention to the pain in my heart and whispered, "I let go." Then I imagined what it would feel like to be free of my hurt. I spent an hour feeling the pain, whispering my release, and imagining my hurt lessening.

The next day, something had shifted. I felt lighter.

It's not easy to do, but sometimes all we can do is let go.

DAY 49: **AN OPENING**

 Heartbreak breaks your heart.

But that break also creates an opening for you to grow.

Don't rush to fill that opening. Let it be open and broken a little longer.

Can you breathe into the tender space?

Can you see how this heartbreak might be the very opening you needed to expand into a fuller version of yourself?

(Hint: Heartbreak is an ending and a new beginning all at once.)

DAY 50: **COMING SOON...**

 There will come a day when you will feel so adored and so seen and so at ease and so supported and so safe, and you will wish that you could run backward in time to when you felt so invisible and so misunderstood and so worried and so excluded and so scared so that you could wrap your arms around that tender younger self and assure her, "Hold on, girl, it's coming."

DAY 51: **PRAY**

 You can pray.

Your prayers do not need to be elaborate speeches or passionate requests to an all-knowing god.

Your prayers can simply be the deepest feelings in your heart— your longing, your gratitude, your uncertainty, your hope—sent silently and sincerely into the sky with faith that they will be caught and answered with love.

DAY 52: **MOON**

 Have you noticed the moon? Its shape and size? Have you watched it arc across the sky?

When it shines down on you with its white light, do you swoon?

Have you ever seen the moon at night only to wake up and see it again the next morning? This is possible, you know.

DAY 53: **REAL + BEAUTIFUL + PERFECT**

 Your body is perfect. Your body is beautiful.

Perhaps you are rolling your eyes right now, ready to list your flaws.

The truth is, however, those "flaws" are not flaws at all. It is our culture that is flawed. Social media is flawed. It is filtered and altered images that are flawed.

So much of what we see is false and fake. So much of what we are encouraged to be is false and fake. False things are lies. Fake things are lies. Lies are the flaws.

True things are the beautiful things. True things are the perfect things.

Your body is real and your body is true, so it cannot be flawed.

Your body is real and so it is beautiful. Your body is real and so it is perfect.

DAY 54: **NOTICE THE WINDOW**

 Find a widow that you can easily look out without interruption. Maybe it's a window in your bedroom or at a library. Any size window will do.

Set a clock for ten minutes.

Look out the window for ten minutes. Do not check your phone during that time.

Notice what you see on the other side of the window. Pay attention to the entire space available to your eyes, right up to the edges.

You don't have to do anything other than observe. When ten minutes are up, stay longer if you'd like or go do something else.

DAY 55: **EVENTUALLY**

 Being a teenager can be really hard. It can feel nearly impossible sometimes.

I think of you, dear reader of these pages, and imagine all the struggles you might face. I wish I had a fail-proof plan you could follow to get you through it with ease. I wish I could wrap you in an invisible magic bubble to keep you happy and safe.

Sadly, I don't. And I can't.

But I can assure you that life will get better. Hang in there. Put one foot in front of the next. Go to your soul, the deepest part of yourself. Find comfort and strength there, and trust that it will eventually get better, because it will.

DAY 56: **CREATIVITY**

 We tend to associate creativity with fine arts. We reserve the label "creative" for painters, musicians, actors, novelists, photographers, and fashion designers, but you can be creative without necessarily being an artist.

All humans are creative. It's very natural, like walking. It is through our creative ingenuity that we humans have grown and adapted throughout the centuries.

You might not be in touch with your creativity, but it is there. Your creativity is simply imagination and curiosity. Your creativity isn't only useful in creating a work of art. It is essential for helping you dream of your highest goals, for solving problems, and creating the type of world you want to live in.

Creativity is a skill like no other. It is a way of viewing and interacting with the world. Can you notice your own creativity, imagination, and curiosity now?

DAY 57: **YOU + THEM**

 You are you. They are them.

And you never really truly know what's going on inside of them.

Usually the images people paint for the outside world to see are not fully detailed pictures of the whole entire story of their lives. They might appear confident and happy, but actually feel insecure and worried.

You be you. Let them be them.

Be kind to both of you.

DAY 58: **TO QUOTE NIKKI GIOVANNI**

 "If you don't understand yourself, you don't understand anybody else."

These words are from Nikki Giovanni, a poet, activist, and educator.

What does this quote mean to you? Why would she say it is necessary to understand yourself before you can understand somebody else? How do we come to understand ourselves? Write freely in your journal or on a piece of paper about how you interpret her words.

DAY 59: **EMOTIONS ARE NEUTRAL**

 There are no "good" emotions or "bad" emotions. Emotions are mostly neutral, natural responses to the events and circumstances of life. Emotions are teachers offering lessons and guidance to more deeply understand your inner life.

Feelings like sadness and anger are not *bad*, but they are definitely uncomfortable and tricker to navigate than feelings of joy. The goal is not to avoid, ignore, numb, or fix these challenging emotions, but to learn how to work with them.

Challenging emotions are not typically navigated easily or quickly. Working with uncomfortable feelings requires a certain amount of bravery, gentle persistence, and faith. It requires that you have lots of tools and resources to care for yourself and get the support you need when you need it.

Today consider the idea that emotions are neutral. If you feel a challenging emotion swell up inside you, can you try not to label it as "bad," but instead simply observe it and do what you need to do to move through it?

DAY 60: **THOUGHTS VS. EMOTIONS**

 Thoughts and emotions are different things. Did you know this?

It is common to get them confused, and you'll know that you've done that if you ever hear yourself say something along the lines of, "I feel like Claire doesn't like me."

Claire doesn't like me is not an emotion. *Claire doesn't like me* is a thought. Most often when we say, "I feel like..." the word *like* is followed by a thought, not an emotion.

Emotions are psychological feelings. Thoughts are your interpretations of situations. It matters that you understand the difference, because if you have your thoughts and emotions jumbled and confused, it makes knowing yourself and being in charge of your own behavior nearly impossible.

A truer way of expressing the sentiment above would be, "I think that Claire doesn't like me, and I feel sad about that." Make sense?

Can you notice the difference between your thoughts and emotions today?

DAY 61: UNTANGLING THOUGHTS FROM EMOTIONS

Your best friend has pulled away from you, ignoring all your attempts to reach out. Your crush has made it clear that the feelings are not mutual. A classmate said something cruel to you in front of everybody.

When these things happen, it's natural to feel all kinds of hard emotions, but it's important not to make your emotions worse with negative thoughts.

In any given situation, there are the emotions *and* there are the thoughts. Thoughts can influence emotions and vice versa, but they are different.

In the above scenarios, your emotions might be embarrassment, fury, confusion, or fear.

Your thoughts, on the other hand, might be something like, "I don't belong. People don't like me. I am not attractive. I will always be lonely."

AMANDA FORD

Do you notice the emotions you feel today? Can you observe the thoughts you have about these emotions? Can you begin to untangle the two?

DAY 62: **SPEAKING EMOTIONS**

Below are some examples of how you can begin to think and speak to help untangle your emotions and your thoughts.

"My friend didn't respond to my text and I feel worried, because I think it means that she is ignoring me."

"My boyfriend broke up with me and I feel heartbroken, because I had dreamed we would be together forever."

"My dad yelled at the waitress and I feel embarrassed, because I think that's rude."

Here's the formula: What Happened (these are the simplest facts about the situation) + How You Feel (your emotion) + The Thought You Are Having or Story You Are Telling.

Writing Prompt: Write about five different circumstances in your life. They can be from the past or the present. Can you identify what happened, what you felt and what you thought you had or story you told about the situation?

DAY 63: **YOU ARE NOT YOUR FEELINGS**

Here's a small shift you can make in your thinking and speaking that can have big impacts on the way you feel about and view yourself.

When talking and thinking about your emotions instead of saying, "I *am* sad," try saying, "I *feel* sad."

You are not your emotions. You are a human being, much bigger and much more complex than a few simple emotions.

Emotions are like weather, passing through you and changing all the time. They do not define you any more than thunderstorms define our earth. Weather shifts and changes, but earth remains. In the same way, your emotions shift and change, but you remain.

Saying *I feel* instead of *I am* to describe your emotions creates space between yourself and them, reminding you that no feeling state is a permanent condition.

DAY 64: **BEAT**

 You want to slip your hand in his back pocket...press your cheek to his chest...inhale. Instead you watch as he dances, his fingers in some other girl's hair, and you grip your chest and wonder if you will ever breathe again.

You want to eat dinner at the table with her mother, her brother, and her dog sitting under your feet. But she walks home with someone else. So you stand at the counter in your kitchen twisting noodles on your fork, and when your dad asks why you aren't eating, you just shrug.

They say the heart wants what it wants. When it doesn't get what it wants, it seems it is certain to stop.

But here's the truth that you must know: Broken hearts still beat, still beat, still beat.

Broken hearts still beat.

DAY 65: **THE BREAKUP CURE**

Each of your first major break-ups will likely feel akin to a death. Your heart will feel as though it is literally, actually, physically broken. That's how badly it will hurt. Your body will ache. Your head will be foggy.

There is only one cure for a breakup: time.

While you can certainly support and care for yourself as your heart heals, time is the only true cure. You cannot rush it or plan it or expect it to go in a straight line. Healing a broken heart has its own schedule.

Be patient with your heart when it hurts. Be patient with your mind when it is slow. Be patient with your body when it aches.

Be patient and trust that time is working its medicine.

DAY 66: **HEARTBREAK HOPES**

With every breakup, there are always two losses: the loss of companionship and the loss of hope. Whether we realize it or not, relationships bring with them the hope that we have finally found true love and a permanent place to belong.

When we grieve a breakup, we mourn not only for what we have lost, but also for what could have been, for a future we imagined for ourselves, a future free of loneliness. This is why sometimes a breakup with somebody we didn't date very long can feel so painful. Sometimes our sadness is more about the loss of hope than it is about the specific person.

When you find yourself in the midst of heartbreak, try to name some of the hopes you had placed on that relationship and understand that saying goodbye to those hopes is a part of your grieving process.

DAY 67: **KIND GOODBYES**

 When the friendship ends, when the relationship dies, you don't have to cause a fight as you go your separate ways.

This isn't a courtroom battle. You don't have to build a case against them.

You don't have to announce your grievances to every person you see.

You can part ways and still be loving, even if they aren't. You can take the high road.

You can wish them well.

You can give a kind goodbye.

DAY 68: **SELF-COMFORT**

Self-comfort is the ability to soothe and care for yourself when times get hard.

Self-comfort is a positive action that moves you closer to healing and wholeness. Self-comfort is not zoning out, numbing out, or hurting yourself.

Self-comfort is about making a conscious choice to do the things that help you calm down and regain a sense of peace. Self-comfort is also about a conscious choice NOT to do the things that make you feel more agitated, more upset, or more hopeless.

Because you are a human in this crazy world, and because this crazy world is full of all sorts of unexpected and painful challenges, you will need to rely on your ability to comfort yourself on many occasions. There might be periods in your life when you need to comfort yourself every single day. No matter how old you are, there will always be times when you need to exercise your skills of self-comfort.

DAY 69: **SELF-COMFORT TOOLKIT**

 Sometimes when we are in the midst of hard emotions, we can forget how to comfort ourselves. This is a catch-22, because it is when we are in the midst of hard emotions that we need our self-comfort skills the most.

Make a list of all the things that help you calm down. Remember that destructive behaviors like smoking weed or scrolling through social media for hours do not count as self-comfort. These things are actually self-destructive.

Write down all the activities that soothe you, everything from listening to music to reading an uplifting book to talking to somebody you trust to petting your cat. Be as specific and thorough as you can. You can add new things to the list when they come to mind.

Keep this list in your journal or anywhere where you can easily find it. The next time you find yourself feeling down, get it out and take action on at least one of the things on this list.

DAY 70: **SAY IT TO YOURSELF**

 What are the magic words that you wish somebody would say to you?

I believe in you. I see your talents, your skills, your smarts. You've got this. I love your smile, your laugh, the color of your eyes. Look how well you did just there! You smell good. You're funny. I like you.

Say these things to yourself. Do it. Right now.

I believe in you. I see your talents, your skills, your smarts. You've got this. I love your smile, your laugh, the color of your eyes. Look how well you did just there! You smell good. You're funny. I like you.

Sometimes we have to say to ourselves the very things we wish others would say to us.

DAY 71: **SAD SONGS ON REPEAT**

 Often it is helpful to talk to your friends about your heartbreak and disappointment, about the things you are angry about and hurt by.

Sometimes, however, talking to friends about these things can turn into a complaint fest. Simply replaying over and over again the injustices done to you will not help you move forward. Picking at the wound will not help you heal. It will only make things worse.

Can you catch yourself when you are being a broken record playing sad songs on repeat? Can you move the needle? Can you sing a new tune?

DAY 72: **NOTICE YOUR FAVORITE COLORS**

 Look for your favorite colors as you go about your day.

Pause when you see them. Take note. Pay attention.

What is the item sporting your favorite colors? A car? A flower? A pair of shoes? A wall?

If you want, take pictures of these items that appear in your favorite color. Create a special folder on your phone or computer for them. It will be fun to look back in a year or two from now and see how many different things you have seen in your favorite colors.

DAY 73: **TO QUOTE SANDRA CISNEROS**

 "Revenge only engenders violence, not clarity and true peace. I think liberation must come from within."

These words are from Sandra Cisneros, a writer.

What does this quote mean to you? Do you agree with her sentiment? How might one find liberation within oneself? Write freely in your journal or on a piece of paper about how you interpret her words.

DAY 74: **THINGS TO TELL YOURSELF WHEN YOU ARE FEELING HARD EMOTIONS**

 It's okay that I feel this way.

This is a normal and natural human emotion.

It makes sense that I feel this way.

I will allow myself to feel all my feelings, no matter how uncomfortable they might be.

Everybody feels this way sometimes.

These feelings won't last forever.

I will give myself extra special care until these feelings pass.

DAY 75: **PURPOSE**

 The purpose of life is not to become rich and famous.

The purpose of life is to stay connected to your heart. When you stay connected to your heart, you can express your unique gifts to help leave the world better than you found it.

Below are some writing prompts to help you figure out what it means for you to stay connected to your heart. You don't have to write essays or even complete sentences. Just let your thoughts flow and write whatever comes to mind even if it doesn't make sense.

When I am connected to my heart, I feel...

When I am not connected to my heart, I feel...

If I stayed connected to my heart all the time, my life would be different because I would...

The things that disconnect me from my heart are...

The things that help me stay connected to my heart are...

DAY 76: **NO**

 You can always say *No*.

Even if just three minutes earlier you said *Yes*.

You can change your mind at any time, for any reason.

You can also change your mind for no reason.

No doesn't need a reason. *No* can simply be a feeling.

You don't need to explain it.

You can say *No* from the start or *No* right before the end.

You can say *No* even if you know that it will disappoint someone.

You can say *No* to anything and everything, to anybody
and everyone.

DAY 77: **HELLO, SUNSET**

 Write a letter to the sunset.

Here's mine if you'd like inspiration:

> Hello Sunset,
> My goodness you are stunning! May I take
> you to dinner?
> As always, Me

DAY 78: **CAN YOU LAUGH AT YOURSELF?**

 Can you laugh at yourself?

How do you respond to being teased?

When you do something ridiculous, how much does it bother you
to have other people notice it and laugh at you?

Do you get embarrassed easily?

DAY 79: **DO IT ANYWAY**

 One of my favorite mottos in life is "Do it anyway." I use it whenever I find myself resisting taking action on the things that I know are right for me.

Don't want to clean your room? Do it anyway.

Don't want to do your homework? Do it anyway.

Don't want to exercise? Do it anyway.

Scared to fess up about the lie you told? Do it anyway.

Scared to try out for the team? Do it anyway.

Scared to talk to that person you have a crush on? Do! It! Anyway!

What boring task or scary action have you been putting off? Today is a good day to do it anyway.

DAY 80: **ANGER**

If emotions are teachers, what does anger have for you to learn?

Anger can be a sign that you have been treated unfairly and need to set a boundary. Let's say that your friend tells a secret you shared with her even though she promised that she wouldn't. You're mad and rightfully so. That *was not* cool of her.

Learning how to express anger constructively is an invaluable skill.

First, let the hot feelings work through you. Vigorous exercise can be really helpful. So can writing all your thoughts out on paper.

Second, decide what you want to do. Using the example above, is this a friend you want to keep or not? Is this the first time she's hurt you or the fiftieth time?

If you do want to keep her as your friend, the third step is to tell her how you feel. Say something like, "You told my secret, and I feel furious. I need to be able to trust you if we're going to be friends. I also feel confused, because you promised you wouldn't tell. And I'm embarrassed, because I didn't want anybody else to know that."

DAY 81: **HOW TO GET ANGER OUT**

 Shake it out.

Run it out.

Dance it out.

Write it out.

Exhale it out.

Cry it out.

Sweat it out.

Sing it out.

Whatever you do, get that anger out of your body so that it doesn't poison you.

DAY 82: **BUT WHY ARE YOU REALLY MAD?**

 Sammy got home past her curfew. Her parents grounded her. She was so mad at her parents.

Nicole's grades dropped below the minimum required to play soccer. She got suspended from the team. She was so mad at her coach.

Maria's friend got mad at her for sharing a secret. Maria got mad back at her friend.

Have you ever gotten mad at somebody for something that was actually your fault? Dig beneath the surface, and you might find that you are actually disappointed or embarrassed. You might find that beneath your anger is a lesson for you to learn. You might discover that there are actually options and things within your control that you can do to improve the circumstances.

DAY 83: A LETTER FOR A HARD CONVERSATION

Writing can be a useful tool for helping you have hard conversations with friends, parents, or teachers. Earlier in this book we explored how you can use writing as a tool to get all your anger out.

If you are hurt or angry with somebody, you can also write a letter directly to that person and read it to them. The nervousness associated with a hard conversation you need to have can be overwhelming and prevent you from being able to state your feelings, thoughts, and hopes clearly.

If you are going to write a letter for a hard conversation, keep it simple and kind. This is not a place to vent all your feelings in the same way that you do in your journal or private writings.

State the facts of what happened, how you feel as a result, the thought stories you are telling in your mind about the situation, and how you hope to move forward. It might take you time to craft your letter, even a few days of thinking about it. That is normal. You don't have to get the words exactly right. Simply do your best to express yourself the way you want to.

DAY 84: **UNEXPECTED**

 It is possible for your life to turn out so much more wonderful and interesting and fulfilling than you can ever imagine.

It is possible for next week, next year, next decade, and beyond to surprise you in the most unexpectedly enchanting ways.

DAY 85: **TREE**

 Find a tree. Go to her.

Stand before her. Introduce yourself. Tell her your name.

Do you know what kind of tree she is? If not, try to find out this week.

Ask her, "May I touch you?" Wait for her reply. Her energy will answer. You will feel it.

If she says *yes*, place your hand on her trunk. Can you feel her buzz? It is subtle, but it is there. That's her life force. That vibrating force is the thing that makes her bud and shed leaves, grow taller, grow branches, and heal when she is cut.

This is what you and the tree have in common: She is alive and so are you.

DAY 86: **SOME QUESTIONS**

 Some questions take time to be answered.

Some questions must be lived into, their answers uncovered slowly over time.

Some questions demand strength, a willingness to sit with all the thorny thoughts that come with uncertainty.

Do I belong? Where am I needed? Does my life matter? Am I loved?

Some questions hurt and ask you to be brave enough to stay with that hurt. Don't numb out, don't hide, don't rush to false conclusions.

Some questions call on you to have faith in yourself, in the arc of life.

Some questions ask you to trust that confusion transforms into clarity with time and that even the sharpest sadness can relax into joy.

DAY 87: **FLOWER**

 Here's a writing exercise for you. You're going to love it, but it only works if you do it *exactly* as I tell you. Promise? Okay!

What is your favorite flower? Write the name of it down on a piece of paper. Spend a moment visualizing the flower. Find a picture of it to enhance your mental image if you want. When you are ready, write about your flower as though it is a person, with as many adjectives as you can think of to describe your flower's personality. Use a thesaurus for inspiration.

For example, my favorite flower is a peony, and her personality is playful, bold, generous, loving, lucky, spiritual, bookish, perceptive, resourceful, hardworking, eloquent, assertive, and creative.

Complete the writing exercise before you read any further.

I mean it! Stop! Do not read any more on this page until you have completed the writing exercise above. You promised!

This writing exercise is magic because in describing your favorite flower as a person, you're actually describing yourself. Projecting yourself onto the objects you love is one way your inner thoughts about yourself become clear.

The qualities you ascribed to the flower are the qualities that you know—deep down—exist inside of you.

DAY 88: **WE NEED YOU**

 To be true to yourself means to discover what is uniquely you and to bring that uniqueness into the world in a way that is meaningful to you.

Don't ever forget this truth: We need you to show up as your truest self in the world, to do what you love, and to use your skills to help.

Don't ever stop discovering yourself and expressing yourself.

Keep showing up as yourself. We need you.

DAY 89: **STUMBLE**

 You will stumble in life, but you can get back up.

You will stumble, stumble, stumble, but you're also going to get back up, get back up, get back up.

Hand on your heart, head held high.

You stumble 782 times? Get back up 783 times!

Ouch! BAM! It happened again!

When you stumble, get right back up.

DAY 90: **GOOD AT**

 Quick! Tell me: What are you good at?

Don't be shy. Don't hesitate. Don't be all like, "Oh. I don't know. I'm not really good at anything in particular."

You were born with natural gifts and talents, and it is essential that you know them and claim them. Knowing what you are good at and doing it wholeheartedly is one way you bring your unique light into the world.

Your gifts and talents don't have to be grand. They can be simple things. Very, very simple things. Your gifts and talents are the activities, ideas, and skills that you are naturally drawn to.

So quick! Tell me: What are you good at?

DAY 91: **ANYTHING**

 Anything you want to be good at, you can become good at.

Anything!

While some things will come more naturally to you than others, it doesn't mean that you cannot become good at things that are hard for you.

Telling jokes, making new friends, skateboarding, applying liquid eyeliner, writing computer code...you name it!

All it takes is sticking with it even when it stops being fun, even when it seems like you are not making progress and never will make progress.

Keep practicing day after day, week after week, year after year, and one day you will discover that you are finally good at that thing that you really wanted to be good at.

It will feel like magic, and you will know that it was you who made it happen.

DAY 92: **BE YOU**

 You look how you look and do what you do.

You are who you are and you love who you love.

There is no apology and there is no more to say.

DAY 93: **TO QUOTE ANNE SEXTON**

 "Sometimes the soul takes pictures of things it has wished for, but never seen."

These are the words of Anne Sexton, a poet.

What does her quote mean to you? How can a soul wish for things it has never seen? Can you relate to this experience? Write freely in your journal or on a piece of paper about how you interpret her words.

DAY 94: **DEEP DOWN**

 Deep down, there is a part of you that knows exactly what to do.

Deep down, there is a part of you that knows your most private dreams, the dreams you are almost too afraid to admit to yourself for fear they are too grand and you are too small. Deep down, there is a part of you that knows these dreams can come true for you.

Deep down, there is a part of you that never forgot how lovable you are.

Deep down, there is a part of you that is not afraid to speak up, not afraid to be alone, not afraid at all.

Deep down, there is a part of you that speaks quietly through gut feelings, instincts, and secret longings. This is the same part of you that existed when you were a baby and the same part of you that will be there when you are an old lady. She is your highest self, your true self, your enduring self.

She is a part of you, and she knows exactly what to do.

DAY 95: **GOOD MORNING, WORLD**

 What might you say to the world upon waking? Write the world a note.

This one's mine:

Good morning, strange World,
I look forward to the adventures you have
*   waiting for me today.*
As always, Me

DAY 96: **SEEING CLEARLY**

 She always felt worse after spending time with her group of friends. This realization struck her like a lightning bolt while walking home after spending the day with them.

For the most part, she felt happy and content in her life. She loved her family and enjoyed her time at home. She liked reading and cooking and helping her dad in the yard. She even liked taking care of her little sister. When she was at home, doing her own thing, she felt at peace, but every time she got together with her friends, she ended up feeling more lonely than she did when she was actually alone.

Her friends were often sarcastic and jokingly putting each other down. They were slightly competitive and didn't really listen to each other. She wasn't sure why she suddenly saw it all so clearly, but once she did, she knew it was time to move on, to make new friends.

And that's what she did.

DAY 97: **UNFAIR**

 Life is not fair. It never has been, and I don't know if it ever will be.

Life is not fair, and that's not fair.

You can hit your head against the wall. You can throw things across the room. You can bruise your own skin or pull out your hair, but none of that will change the fact that life is not fair. It never has been. It probably never will be.

It's not fair, but you can still choose to do your best with what you've got.

DAY 98: **EASY WAY OUT**

 Sometimes it can be tempting to take the lazy, easy way out, to zone out, to goof off, to ignore responsibility and escape into instant gratification and distraction.

Sometimes it's okay to take the lazy, easy way out. Keep in mind: *Sometimes* does not mean *most of the time.*

It might feel good in the moment, but evading responsibilities will make your life much harder down the road. It might be hard for you to imagine the future, but it is up ahead waiting for you. You will get to the future eventually, so set yourself up for a successful arrival.

The ability to think beyond the immediate moment, to work first and play second, is a skill worth cultivating. Can you notice the ways in which you check out? Are there certain situations in which you are more likely to want to avoid doing what needs to be done?

DAY 99: **SAMENESS**

 What if all music sounded the same?

What if all food tasted the same?

What if all movies told the same story?

What if there was one type of flower, one type of animal, only one color?

Now think about somebody you know, maybe a good friend or your cousin or your good friend's cousin.

Now imagine that everybody in the world—including you—is exactly like that person. Seriously envision it. Can you picture what it would be like if everybody looked, sounded, thought, and moved identically?

What a strange and boring world that would be.

DAY 100: **DRAW CIRCLES**

 Get out a pen and piece of paper and draw circles. Draw them all over the margins of this book if you'd like. Or draw them right on top of these very words.

Drawing helps activate the feel-good parts of your brain, so if you are feeling worried, bored, confused, edgy, stuck, or any other feeling that is hard to deal with, drawing can be one tool to help you feel better. Circles are a super simple shape that you can draw even if you "can't draw."

Simply draw circles over and over. Or draw one big circle and then a smaller circle inside it, and then an even smaller one and another smaller one.

Draw circles with your nondominant hand.

Draw circles in a pattern. Or make them totally random.

Color them if you'd like. Or not. There are no rules.

DAY 101: **BOOBS**

 Speaking of circles, aren't boobs cool?

There are so many different types. Some look like balloons and some look like teardrops. Some bounce and some stay still. Some are curvy. Some are flat. Nipples can point up or out or down.

Each girl's body is unique and distinct in its own way.

It's kind of cool if you really think about it. There are billions of girls and women in the world, and although we have similar parts, those parts look different on each of us.

Instead of wishing for your body to look different than it does, instead of trying to mold your body to look like somebody else's, can you appreciate your body for its uniqueness? Can you appreciate the differences in others and see just how cool it is that there is infinite variety?

DAY 102: **YOUR BODY IS YOUR HOME**

 Throughout your life, you might live in many houses, many cities, or many countries, but you will only live in one body. Your body is your lifetime home.

Your body is the container that holds your hurts and your joys. It is the thing that lets you hug and hold hands and feel the breeze and taste food and read books and hear music and see the moon. It is the vessel through which you experience life. From the painful to the mundane to the glorious, your body takes part in it all.

Your body, exactly as it looks and feels in this very moment, is worthy of every ounce of devotion, delight, and care that you can lavish upon it. I hope you know this.

Your body is your home. Treat it well.

DAY 103: **TAKING CARE OF YOUR BODY**

 Taking care of your body is simpler than you might expect, and a little bit of basic care goes a long way.

Here are the basics of body care:

- Move your body every day in a way that feels good to you.
- Get enough sleep.
- Drink plenty of water, and eat as well as you can most of the time, but don't obsess about eating perfectly.
- Floss your teeth.
- Get into nature as often as possible.
- Think kindly of your body. Speak kindly about your body.

DAY 104: **MOVE YOUR BODY**

 Move your body every day in a way that feels good to you.

This doesn't necessarily need to be sports or exercise. If you like sports and exercise, great. If not, you don't have to force yourself to do something you hate in order to get the benefits of movement.

Movement is the natural state of your body. Your body is built to move.

It could be a simple stretch of reaching your arms to the sky, a walk around the block, dancing in your bedroom, skipping in a field, climbing a tree, planting and pulling weeds in a community garden, or swimming.

Movement doesn't have to be vigorous. It doesn't have to last long. The only rule is that it must feel good to *you*. Can you find a movement you enjoy? Can you do a little bit every day?

DAY 105: **MOVEMENT DOESN'T HAVE TO BE SPORTS**

 Movement and exercise are so often associated either with competitive sports or with weight loss and trying to mold our bodies to fit into an ever-changing, unattainable "ideal."

This is too bad, because these ways of thinking about movement and exercise turn many people away from moving their bodies at all.

You don't have to play sports or try to lose weight in order to have a meaningful relationship with movement and exercise.

Movement and exercise help you regulate your emotions, think more clearly, develop your brain, keep all your organs functioning, sleep better, and have more energy.

Can you think of ways that movement and exercise help make your life better?

DAY 106: **YOUR BODY**

 Your body is your own.

May you get to know it well.

May you learn what it likes.

May you take delight in those likes.

Your body belongs to you and you deserve to know it well.

And you deserve to take delight.

DAY 107: **DRAWING EXPERIMENT**

 You'll need a paper and pen for this.

Observe something in your immediate vicinity. A mug. Your friend's shoes. A bouquet of flowers. Your sandwich.

Look at it carefully for a few minutes.

Pick up the pen with your nondominant hand, close your eyes, and draw the object.

Recreate the details as best you can, but don't stress about trying to make your drawing look realistic. Enjoy the process of feeling the pen move across the page.

This is an experiment about learning to enjoy the process, not stressing about the final product. Kind of like life, huh?

DAY 108: **BLUE BODY**

 When you bump your leg and get a bruise, it hurts and it can turn blue.

Have you ever noticed that when you have the emotional blues your body can hurt, too?

Sadness, loneliness, melancholy, and hopelessness can make you tired, nauseous, and achy. Feelings can change your appetite and make it hard to think.

When you have a physical wound, you do the things you need to encourage your body to heal. You use ice, ointments, band-aids, wraps, splints, casts. You might eat special foods that help you feel better. You might take medicine. You rest and give it time.

Your emotional hurts are similar to a broken finger in that they don't magically heal overnight. They need care and they take time.

DAY 109: **SENSATIONS**

 Sensations are all the physical feelings you experience using your five senses.

Being aware of your body sensations can help you in all sorts of ways, from working with difficult emotions to coping with physical pain and injury. When you are in a challenging situation where you feel nervous, embarrassed, extremely sad, or overwhelmed, simply tuning into your physical sensations can help you stay grounded and calm.

Here are some words that describe physical sensations:

Hot. Warm. Cold. Tingly. Sharp. Soft. Smooth. Ticklish. Buzzing. Itchy. Twitchy. Hollow. Numb. Tight. Constricted. Achy. Heavy. Relaxed. Pounding. Cozy. Glowing. Raw. Throbbing. Nauseous. Fluttery. Wobbly. Rough. Spacious. Neutral. Piercing. Blocked. Flowing. Sweaty. Knotted. Bubbly. Radiant. Dizzy. Spacey. Hollow. Sore.

How many of these sensations can you feel in your body right now? Can you notice different sensations as they arise in your body throughout the day? Can you think of other sensations not on this list?

DAY 110: **BODY SCAN**

 Here's a practice you can do to help you become more aware of your body sensations. You can use this practice as a way to unwind before sleep, as a way to calm your nerves before doing something challenging like giving a presentation, or simply as a way to get to know yourself better.

This practice is typically done while lying down, but you can do it in any position you'd like, as long as you are comfortable.

You will move through your body, pausing at various points along the way and noticing the sensations you feel. Start at your toes, then move to your feet, then your ankles, shins, knees, thighs, hips, lower back, upper back, shoulders, upper arms, elbows, forearms, wrists, hands, and fingers. Then go forward, up to your eyes, nose, cheeks, lips, neck, chest, and finally your belly.

Simply notice the sensations in your body at each place you pause. If you notice your attention wandering, simply bring it back to the present moment.

You cannot do this practice incorrectly, so don't feel pressure to do it "right."

DAY 111: **DEAR BODY**

 Write a letter to your body. Use the following prompts for inspiration. Don't overthink it. Write freely and roam in whatever directions come naturally, even if it doesn't make sense.

Dear Body, I am thankful that you...

Dear Body, I'm sorry that I...

Dear Body, I'm sorry that the world...

Dear Body, I wish that you knew...

Dear Body, I know that you are happy and healthy when...

Dear Body, I know that you are sad and unhealthy when...

Dear Body, how will I know if...

DAY 112: **A PRACTICE FOR BEING KINDER TO YOUR BODY**

Try this practice either in the shower, while looking in a mirror, or while lying on your bed before sleep.

Look at your feet. Say, "Hello, feet. I see you. I feel you. Thank you."

Look at your legs. Say, "Hello, legs. I see you. I feel you. Thank you."

Look at your belly. Say, "Hello, belly. I see you. I feel you. Thank you."

Look at your hands. Say, "Hello, hands. I see you. I feel you. Thank you."

Look at your breasts. Say, "Hello, breasts. I see you. I feel you. Thank you."

Do this for every part of your body with which you feel comfortable. Do this every day or once a week or once a month or once a year. Make sure you at least do it once in your lifetime.

DAY 113: **BODY TALK**

 If you have been holding negative thoughts about your body, it might be hard to start immediately having kind thoughts toward it. You can, however, learn to think about your body in neutral terms.

When you find yourself thinking, "My thighs are too fat," can you replace that statement with something neutral like, "Those are my thighs. They help me stand up and sit down."

When you think, "My skin is ugly," replace it with "This is my skin. It protects my organs, and it feels good when it is touched."

If you struggle to think something kind about your body, can you at least try to change the mean thoughts to neutral ones?

DAY 114: **LIGHT**

 Keep your light shining, dear girl.

You never know who is looking to you for guidance in the dark.

Let your light out. Don't dim it to please anybody. Don't let anybody dim it for you.

Where is the spark inside you? What lights you up and keeps your light alive in the world?

Find brighter friends if you need to. Create a brighter world if you need to.

DAY 115: **NOT ALONE**

 You are not alone.

You are not alone.

You are not alone.

Somewhere in this big wide world there is somebody who is going through almost the exact same thing that you are going through.

Somewhere in this big wide world there is somebody else who already went through almost the exact same thing that you are going through and who is on the other side and who is stronger and better now.

DAY 116: **SEEKING BEAUTY**

 Humans seek beauty. We are drawn to it. We search for sunsets and sprawling vistas, admire them in awe, soak them in. We grow flowers and smell flowers and arrange flowers in vases. We savor art. We decorate our spaces. We adorn ourselves.

True beauty inspires us and makes life richer. It reminds us that being alive is incredible.

Beauty becomes shallow and meaningless only when we reduce it down to a very narrow set of ideas, when we think of it only in terms of a specific sort of physical attractiveness, when we allow other people to dictate to us what is beautiful and what is not.

AMANDA FORD

What is beautiful to you? Where do you see beauty around you? What sounds or even smells beautiful? Have you ever created something beautiful? Can you extend your search for beauty to *yourself*? Find some beauty on the inside and outside of you.

DAY 117: **TO QUOTE MAE JEMISON**

 "Never limit yourself because of others' limited imagination; never limit others because of your own limited imagination."

These words come from Mae Jemison, an American engineer, physician, and former NASA astronaut who was the first Black woman to travel into space.

What does her quote mean to you? Have you ever felt limited by other people's opinions of you? Do you think you have ever limited another person by your opinion of them? Write freely in your journal or on a piece of paper about how you interpret her words.

DAY 118: **COLOR**

 Have you ever noticed how colors can evoke feelings and thoughts?

When you really like a color, you are drawn to it. You get a feeling when you look at it. The feeling might be very subtle and hard to put into words, but you can feel it.

When you really do not like a color, you get a different feeling. Have you ever had to wear a piece of clothing when you really did not like its color? Do you remember how it made you feel?

Notice the colors in your world today. Do any of them make you feel a particular way? This exercise might seem pointless, but it offers you a glimpse of your preferences and of how you instinctually pull toward and pull away from certain things.

In the same way that colors evoke subtle feelings and pulls for you, certain people, places, ideas, and activities will do the same. These subtle feelings and attractions are some of the clues your highest self uses to guide you toward her.

DAY 119: **YOU MIGHT THINK**

 You might think you need to say something clever, something smart.

You might think you need to be certain and show what you know.

You do not.

It is enough to feel the swell of your heart at the mere thought of the things you love.

DAY 120: **GO BABY GIRL!**

 Have you ever watched a baby learn to walk? They take one step, maybe two or three, and then fall to the ground. Everybody cheers for the baby. "Look at you! You've got it! Yay! You're walking!"

Technically, the baby isn't walking. The baby is *learning to walk.* Even so, everybody is thrilled. People were likely thrilled in this way when you took your first steps.

This support likely dwindled as you grew older and people around you became more interested in evaluating your end result:

AMANDA FORD

Did you earn a good grade, did you make the goal, did you win the award?

But you are like a baby in so many things. You are like a baby in anything new that you are doing, whether it's algebra, drawing, skateboarding, or kissing.

Encourage your inner baby as she learns. Encourage her even as she falls flat on her face. Go, baby girl, go!

DAY 121: CAN YOU FEEL IT?

 There is a heartbeat inside the earth.

You can feel it if you get down on your hands and knees in the grass.

You can feel it if you stand with your bare feet in the dirt.

You can feel it if you drape your body over a boulder.

You can feel it if you wrap your arms around a tree.

You can feel it if you lie in the sand with your limbs spread like a star.

DAY 122: CHOOSE WHO YOU WANT TO BE

 Every day you get to choose who you want to be.

While there are some parts of yourself that you have no control over (your height, for example), you do have 100 percent control over your character, the way you conduct yourself, and how you treat others.

Your friends and family will act in certain ways and, while you might value many of their characteristics, you may value different things as well.

You can help yourself get clear about the type of person you want to be by making a list of the character traits you value. A thesaurus can help with this.

Here are some of my words. Take any that apply and add your own.

Authentic, earnest, honest, present, enthusiastic, intellectually curious, discerning, clever, centered, strong, healthy, optimistic, clear, pragmatic, spontaneous, flexible, artistic, expressive, devoted, trustworthy, inspiring, playful, patient, loving.

DAY 123: **EVOLUTION**

A curveball thrown from life's left field can send you in an exciting new direction.

A failure can shed light on something you hadn't seen before.

A slump can give way to a burst of energy.

A loss can create space for something you've always dreamed of to grow.

The key is to hang in there long enough for life's mystery to work its magic.

DAY 124: **TRUE FRIENDS**

 The secret to developing true friendships is allowing yourself to be seen as you truly are. You must be truthful about who you are, your values, what you're into and what you're not.

Being truthful doesn't mean you need to reveal all your secrets, be blunt or rude in your opinions, or share all your feelings with somebody you just met.

Being truthful means not pretending to like things that you don't actually like, not claiming to know things that you don't actually know, and not doing things that you don't actually want to do.

If you want true friends, you have to start by living the truth of who you are.

DAY 125: **RULE 1 FOR MAKING GOOD FRIENDS**

 If you want good friends in your life, you have to start by being a good friend.

Show interest in getting to know about your friends' outer lives and inner lives. Remember important things they share with you. Follow up. Check in.

See the good in them. Say what you see. Let your friends know all the amazing qualities you see in them. Reflect their beauty back to them.

Be there when they are down.

Give them space to breathe. Don't be jealous or possessive of people. Give your friends room to be themselves.

DAY 126: **RULE 2 FOR MAKING GOOD FRIENDS**

 If you want good friends in your life, you absolutely must choose only those people who can be a good friend to you. Not everyone is capable of true friendship. Some people are self-absorbed, unkind, and like to cause drama.

A good friend will show interest in knowing the real you, will remember things you say, will follow up on those things, and will check in.

A good friend will see the good in you, tell you what they see, and reflect all your beauty and amazing qualities back at you. You will feel better about yourself in their presence.

A good friend will be there for you when you are down.

A good friend will give you space to breathe and let you be yourself. They will not be jealous or possessive of you.

DAY 127: **RELIEF**

 Her friends were laughing and joking. They were together, five of them, hanging out in the basement.

She watched the smiles on her friends' faces and heard their boisterous laughter. She wanted to join in, but for some reason she wasn't in the mood and so sat quietly in the corner.

When one of her friends quipped, "What's wrong with you?" she burst into tears.

"I don't know," she said. "I just feel sad. I have no idea why."

AMANDA FORD

Her friend went to her and hugged her. "Oh. Wow. You know what? I kind of feel the same, and I'm sort of just pretending to be happy hoping it will make me feel better."

Maybe that moment didn't solve everything, but the shared understanding did offer some relief for her. It was nice to know that she had friends in the same boat.

DAY 128: **TELLING STORIES**

 Your friend ignores your text.

What does it mean?

Does it mean she's mad at you? Does it mean she's self-absorbed and thoughtless? Does it mean she lost her phone? Does it mean she broke her leg and is in the hospital? Does it mean she's in trouble with her parents? Does it mean she's focused on her homework? Does it mean she's just not in the mood to talk because she's feeling the blues? Does it mean something else entirely?

We tell stories about events in order to give them meaning to us, but can you see how one small action can have many different interpretations?

Can you see how it might be best to wait, to not create a solid story in your mind until you know for sure what is going on?

DAY 129: **LET OTHERS TEACH YOU**

 Have you ever suspected that somebody doesn't like you? Has a friend ever pulled away from you unexpectedly?

While it is important not to let your feelings of self-worth be dependent on other people's opinions of you, sometimes there might be something for you to learn in these sorts of situations.

If you are interested and feel brave enough to engage, you can always ask, "Did I do something to upset you?" (If you don't feel safe or ready to ask this question of the other person, that's okay.)

Sometimes a person won't like you because of something mean or thoughtless you did without realizing it. We aren't always aware of how our own behavior affects others, and it is through social interactions that we develop.

These can be hard conversations to have, but they can also be very helpful. You might learn something new about yourself and potentially steer your relationship with the other person in a new direction.

DAY 130: **APOLOGIZING**

 When a friend lets you know that they have been hurt by something you did, hear them out. As tempting as it might be to defend or explain yourself, don't do that just yet. Listen. Take in what they are saying.

When you have heard them, ask yourself, "Is there anything for me to learn from this situation? Is there anything for me to apologize for?"

Sometimes people get mad at us for reasons that have nothing to do with us, but usually there is something we can learn when somebody we care about is upset with us.

When we recognize that something we did was hurtful, it is in our own best interest to take responsibility. Verbally acknowledging

AMANDA FORD

what you did and apologizing when necessary will not only build a bridge between you and the other person, it will also help you to know yourself better and keep you from repeating the same mistakes over and over again.

DAY 131: **DISAGREE**

 Some people will not understand you. Some people will pressure you to think what they think and do what they do. People always like it better when you agree with them.

But you won't always agree with everybody. The fact that you have an opinion, a perspective, and a stance of your own is a good thing. Don't change yourself to please others. Don't be a chameleon in order to ease the tension of disagreement.

Let there be tension. Let yourself disagree. Let them be annoyed.

And remember that the flip side is also true: People don't always have to agree with you.

When you find yourself in disagreement, try these lines and see how they work: I disagree, but I still like you. I don't want to do that, but I still want to be your friend.

Walk away if you must. Change the subject if you must, but don't contort yourself in order to be in complete agreement with somebody else. Doing that is a kind of lie, and lies never work.

Someday you might change your mind. Or they might change their mind. In the meantime, it's okay to disagree.

DAY 132: **WRITING A NEW ENDING**

 Can you think of a time when you acted in a way that you weren't proud of or said something you wish you hadn't?

Write freely about a time like this. Write the details of the situation, the outcome, and how you felt about it.

Now, write the situation as if you had behaved in a way that was aligned with your highest values. What would have done differently? How would your behavior have changed the outcome?

There's no shame in making mistakes, especially if you learn from mistakes. One great way to learn is to revisit the situation and visualize yourself making different choices. The purpose is not to punish yourself, but simply to help yourself see other options so that the next time you are in a similar situation, you won't make the same mistakes.

DAY 133: **EMOTIONS FLOW**

 See your emotions as clouds floating by in the sky; watch them come and go with the breeze.

See your emotions as a river. Sometimes the rapids will churn fiercely. Sometimes the water will be calm and clear. Either way, let it flow. Don't get caught on a crag. Don't dam it up.

See your emotions as seasons shifting in time. Summer always relaxes into fall. Winter always blooms back into spring.

DAY 134: **THE BLUES**

 She called her mom from school. "What's up, baby?" her mom asked.

"I don't know," she said.

"Did something happen? What's wrong?" her mom asked.

"No. I don't know," she said.

"You're just feeling sad?" her mom asked.

"I guess," she said.

"Oh, sweetie. Sometimes the blues just wash over us and there's nothing much to do. Keep breathing. Get through the day. You can take a bath when you get home, and I'll make you tacos."

Sometimes the blues will wash over you. You can feel blue for no particular reason and every possible reason. Keep breathing. Just get through the day. Take a bath or a shower when you get home. Eat something delicious.

DAY 135: **MEDICINE FOR THE BLUES**

 Place one hand on your chest and one hand on your belly. Can you feel the pulse of your heart? Can you feel the rise and fall of your breath?

Listen to music that makes you feel something. Move your body to the rhythm. Don't worry about trying to dance in a way that looks good. Let your body twitch and sway in whatever way comes up.

Make a sound. Scream. Growl. Wail. Sing. Go somewhere where nobody can hear you if it helps you feel comfortable.

Connect to nature. This can be as simple as placing your hand on a tree on your street.

Eat warm, hearty foods like soup or baked chicken and rice.

Cuddle an animal.

Talk to somebody who has been through it before, like a trusted friend, a school counselor, or your grandmother.

DAY 136: **PAY ATTENTION TO YOUR CLASSROOM**

School demands that you spend time in the same rooms over and over, day after day, year after year. It's easy to get bored and complacent in a space when you believe you know it like the back of your hand.

If you choose to take notice, you can bring a renewed vibrancy to what has become ho-hum.

Notice one new thing every day in your classrooms: a decoration, a place where paint is scuffed and looks like a heart, the texture of the floor, or the variation of color on the ceiling.

You can do this even if you are homeschooling, because it's likely that there are plenty of things around your house that you take for granted because you see them so often.

You can also extend your attention out and begin noticing something new on your way to or from school as well.

DAY 137: **TEETER TOTTER**

 Life is not like a teeter totter where if one person goes up, another person must go down.

If you put someone down, it will not lift you up.

If someone gets lifted up, it will not put you down.

It is possible for us all to go up and up and up and up.

DAY 138: **STICKS AND STONES**

 I remember nearly every awful thing that has been said about me. If I conjure them to mind, the insults still sting; they still fill me with the heat of shame. For much of my young adult life, I accepted these insults and believed that they spoke essential truths about me. I took them in, repeated them to myself in my own mind. I let them shape my self-image and limit my own potential.

Sticks and stones will break your bones, but words will never hurt you...

Unless you let them. The terrible things people say about you only hold power if you grant them power.

It is possible to stop believing and repeating the hurtful things that people say about you. It is not easy, but it is possible with practice.

Start by simply noticing. When you catch yourself thinking cruel things about yourself, pause. Take a breath. Then say to yourself, "I'm sorry, self. I don't want to be mean to you. I want to be kind to you."

The mere intention of wanting to be kind to yourself will set the groundwork for genuine expressions and feelings of kindness toward yourself in the future.

DAY 139: **CYBERBULLYING**

In junior high, I would sit on the bus with my headphones blasting my favorite song on repeat, pretending not to notice the boys who were taunting me. We shared the same stop, but I would rush off before them and sneak between fences to take the long way home through the greenbelt. Once I arrived, I closed the door and let out a sigh of relief that I was safe.

Before the internet and social media, bullying was limited to shared spaces in person. Today, however, bullies can torment you twenty-four hours a day.

My heart goes out to any and everybody who has ever experienced any form of cyberbullying. It is pervasive and can have dire consequences. That's why it's important that you know what it is and how to protect yourself from it.

Before we dive in, let me remind you that cruelty of any sort is never warranted. If you are a victim of any type of cruelty, know that it is not your fault. If you are participating in any type of cruelty toward another person, question yourself as to why you are doing it and do what you can to stop yourself from continuing.

DAY 140: **WHAT IS CYBERBULLYING?**

Cyberbullying is the use of technology to harass, intimidate, or share information (truth or lies) intended to embarrass somebody.

This can include insulting or threatening somebody on a website or blog, posting somebody else's private photos in a public place, spreading a rumor via text or social media, or pretending online to be somebody that you are not in order to trick, tease, or harass somebody else.

Can you think of other forms of cyberbullying? Have you ever witnessed, participated in, or been a victim of cyberbullying?

DAY 141: IT IS A BIG DEAL

 People participate in cyberbullying because they think it's not a big deal, they think they won't get caught, they feel pressured by friends to participate, they think everybody does it, and/or they do not consider the consequences of their actions on the person being bullied.

While it's one thing to have one or two people say something awful to your face, it is quite another to have a whole group of people, many of whom might be cloaking themselves in anonymity, harass you through technology.

Cyberbullying is a type of psychological torture that can have extreme effects on a person's physical and mental health. It is a form of public humiliation that spreads quickly, and it can be hard to escape and difficult, if not impossible, to remove bullying content from the internet.

Cyberbullying is not a harmless activity by "kids just being kids." Whether you are a victim of it or you are participating in it, it is a very hurtful and serious matter.

DAY 142: **PROTECT YOURSELF FROM CYBERBULLYING**

 Do not share the password of your phone or computer with anybody other than your parents.

Keep your personal information, such as email, home address, and phone number, private.

Do not take any photos of yourself that you would be embarrassed if your grandmother or your entire school saw. Even if you think you are just sharing these photos with one person, there is always a chance that those photos can make their way into circulation.

Keep your social media accounts private and only allow people you know and trust to see what you post. Remember that people can easily create fake accounts and not truly be the people they are presenting themselves as.

Do not feed the trolls! If people in a chat room or other online space start being unpleasant, simply log off. Don't begin arguments with people online.

DAY 143: **IF YOU ARE BEING CYBERBULLIED**

 Remember: It's not your fault. It is scary and deeply hurtful, but you can move through it.

You are not alone. There are resources and people who can help you. It is not weak to ask for help.

Tell adults you trust. Talk to the police if needed.

Save messages and screenshots as evidence. Block and report all bullies.

AMANDA FORD

Stop using the platforms where the bullying happened for a few days, a few weeks, or indefinitely.

Spend time in the real world. Pull out all your self-comfort tools. Surround yourself with people you trust and things that make you feel good.

DAY 144: **BEFORE YOU HIT SEND**

 Be careful what you put in a text message, share on social media, or send in an email.

Absolutely nothing you say or send is private once you hit send, no matter how much you trust the person on the other end. Even if you delete something you've posted, it still exists somewhere. Once it's out there, it's out there.

Ask yourself, "Would I be humiliated if my parents saw or read this?" If the answer is yes, *do not hit send*!

Ask yourself, "Would I feel terrible if everybody at my school saw or read this?" If the answer is yes, *do not hit send*!

Ask yourself, "Would the person in this photo be humiliated if their parents saw this?" If the answer is yes, *do not hit send*!

Ask yourself, "Would the person I am talking about have their feelings hurt if they read what I am saying about them?" If the answer is yes, *do not hit send*!

DAY 145: **YOUR POWER**

 You have more power than you realize to make someone's day.

A small gesture, a simple smile, or a kind word or two can change their trajectory from downward to skyward.

You can dismiss and disgrace, you can ignore and show contempt.

Or you can remember that each and every one of us is vulnerable and afraid, each and every one of us longs to be safe, to be seen, to be loved. You can show respect for this.

You likely won't feel love for everybody, but you can infuse each and every action with the awareness of your shared humanity, with your compassion, goodwill, and highest intentions. When you do that, you are more powerful than you realize.

DAY 146: **TO QUOTE GRACE HOPPER**

 "The most damaging phrase in the language is: 'It's always been done that way.'"

These words are from Grace Hopper, an American computer scientist, mathematician, and Navy admiral. She joined the Navy in 1943 and in the 1950s pioneered the idea of machine-independent programming languages, which was the basis for high-level programming languages still in use today.

What does her quote mean to you? Do you agree? Are there things in the world that have "always been done that way" that you think could and should be done differently? Write freely in your journal or on a piece of paper about how you interpret her words.

DAY 147: **WHO YOU ARE**

You are not who you think you are. You are not who others think you are. You are much, much more.

You are not the grades you earn or the clothes you wear.

You are not the list of adjectives your friends use to describe you.

You are not the list of adjectives your enemies use to describe you.

You are not the wave of emotion that floods your mind and heart.

You are not an emoji.

Your body is mostly water, and your body is filled with microscopic bugs.

You breathe in oxygen and breathe out carbon dioxide. The trees around you breathe in your carbon dioxide and breathe oxygen back out for you. How magical is that?

You are supported by the unseen forces of the universe: atmosphere and gravity and many more.

You have a unique fingerprint and you belong here.

DAY 148: **MOTTOS**

 Mottos are pithy sayings to help keep our minds and hearts focused on what matters most. I love mottos and have created many for my own life.

The mottos I most commonly repeat to myself are: Do your best with what you've got. Keep your mind close to home. If you lose your sense of humor, find a new one. It's good luck to be lighthearted. I am stronger than I think I am, and I can do more than I think I can. I can figure out and learn anything and everything that I need to learn. All of life is art. Move your body every day that feels good to you. Feel your breath. Touch nature. Put your highest intentions first. Keep moving.

Collect mottos for yourself. They can be your own words or somebody else's. Write them down and look at them whenever you need reminders of who you are and what you want to be.

DAY 149: **DEAR MOON**

 Write a note to the moon.

Here's mine:

> Dear Moon,
> No matter your size or shape or color or
>   height in the sky, I love you so much,
>   always forever perfectly. And when you
>   shine at me like that the way you always
>   do, I swear to God you love me too.
> Eternally yours, Me

DAY 150: **A CLUE**

 One of my most vivid childhood memories was the day I got my first library card. I was five, and, boy, was I thrilled. Growing up, I spent hours inside the library.

From an early age, I found myself drawn to poetry and philosophy books. I would take them off the shelf and flip through the pages, even though I was too young to understand most of the words and concepts inside. Sometimes I would simply stand and stare at the book titles. There was an energy and an excitement for me just being around those poetry and philosophy books that I didn't feel around the geography or finance books.

As a teen, young adult, and fully grown woman, poetry and philosophy have been essential tools for helping me navigate my life. I couldn't imagine my world without them.

But how did I know this at such a young age? Why was I drawn to those books long before I could even understand them?

What were you drawn to as a young girl? What are you drawn to now? Follow the pull of the energy. It is a clue leading you on the path to your true self.

DAY 151: **HOW TO GET READY IN THE MORNING**

 Step 1: Take a shower.

Step 2: Floss your teeth.

Step 3: Forget every one of the unrealistic expectations and mean beauty standards that are thrust upon girls and women by society.

Step 4: Accept yourself totally.

Step 5: Look in the mirror and say, "Hello, self. It's good to see you. Let's go do this day!"

DAY 152: **NOT TREATED EQUALLY**

 On the first day of class, my high school English teacher told us, "I will not treat you all equally. I will treat you all according to how you conduct yourself in class. If you show up and take pride in your work, I will respect you. You will get freedom to choose your assignments and set your own deadlines. If you slack off and do your work carelessly, you will not be given these freedoms."

This might sound harsh, but it's exactly how things work in the real world. People who work hard, have a good attitude, and keep their word are often given different opportunities than those who do not.

You might not have a choice about many of the circumstances of your life, but you always have a choice about how you conduct yourself inside those circumstances.

DAY 153: SCHOOL

 School is going to be a part of your life for at least a few more years if you are lucky. Yep, that's right: Lucky!

You might enjoy school. If that is true, I am delighted for you.

Or you might hate school or feel somewhat indifferent toward it. If that is true, I am going to encourage you to shift your thoughts just slightly.

School, no matter how boring or seemingly unrelated to your true interests, educates you, both intellectually and socially.

School exposes you to new ideas and encourages you to acquire knowledge and develop skills. It allows you to build upon your strengths and gives you opportunities to improve upon your weaknesses.

School also opens the door for you to learn to work with people that you don't get along with or don't understand. Whether it's a teacher or a classmate, you are bound to bump up against a personality that rubs you the wrong way. Learning to work with these people is a life skill that will carry you far, because life will be full of people that you do not like.

AMANDA FORD

If your feelings about school are blah or negative, I encourage you to open your mind to the possibility that there might be something more in it for you.

DAY 154: **ON CLASSES YOU DON'T LIKE**

 At some point you will likely have to take a class that you don't like.

Whether that class is gym or math, art or science, give it your best anyway.

Be curious. Ask, "What is there for me to learn here?"

Keep an open mind. You might be surprised that you end up gaining something useful. You might be even more surprised that you actually end up liking the class after all.

Put in a sincere effort even when tasks are tedious or seem pointless. Learning to do the hard, boring, monotonous things without complaining or procrastinating is a skill that will serve you well for the rest of your life, because life is full of hard, boring, monotonous tasks. The more willing and able you are to meet these tasks with a good attitude, the happier and more successful you will be.

DAY 155: **SMARTS**

 I like to think of smarts as coming in three different flavors: book smarts, street smarts, and heart smarts.

Book smarts are your intellect. This is your ability to learn and integrate new information. It is your ability to think critically about a topic, to write about it, speak about it, and understand it. Book smarts can be reflected in your grades and test scores.

Street smarts are your life skills. They can be seen in the way you navigate the world: your self-discipline, hard work, and common sense. Street smarts are your ability to make the most of any situation—your imagination and ingenuity. Street smarts are also about your ability to work well with all different types of people.

Heart smarts are your ability to name and manage your emotions. They are your willingness to be present to all your feelings without allowing your feelings to run your life. They are your ability to respond to your emotions instead of reacting from your emotions. Heart smarts include your empathy and compassion for others.

Can you see how these three smarts show up in you?

DAY 156: CREATE A BLACKOUT POEM

 A blackout poem is a poem that you create by crossing out words on a page from a magazine, newspaper, or book using a black pen. You cross out all the words that you don't want in the poem, leaving only the words that you do want to show. Search online for "Blackout Poems" and you'll see lots of examples.

A blackout poem is a fun exploration of discovery. Instead of having to come up with the words all on your own, you pay attention to the words already on the page and connect them by blacking out everything else. It's a puzzle of sorts, and what emerges is something new and different from what was there before.

DAY 157: **INTELLECT**

 Your intellect is your ability to process, remember, and understand information. It is also your ability to think deeply and make complex connections about that information. Your intellect is a part of your inner life.

Your intellect will create opportunities for you and will be the foundation of many accomplishments you make.

Your intellect is not a fixed entity. With commitment, you can become smarter at any point in your life. The cool thing about your teenage years, however, is that this is the time when your brain is primed for learning. Anything you decide to learn will come quicker and will stick around stronger and longer than it will for an adult trying to learn the same material.

This is not the time to skip out on learning. This is the time to develop your intellect by learning everything you can about everything you can. This doesn't mean that you have to be the top of your class. It simply means that now is the time to give your best, most sincere effort to learning new things. Your brain will thank you for it.

DAY 158: **NO MORE THINKING**

 Here's a rule I follow religiously: no thinking when tired, hungry, or sedentary. No good ever comes from thinking under these conditions.

If you are tired or hungry or have been sitting down all day, it'll be a lot harder to figure out the things you're stuck on, such as your math problem, your love life problem, or your family problem.

How do you keep your mind from thinking? Notice that your mind is working and bring it back to the task at hand in the present moment, in this case, caring for your basic needs, whether that's taking a nap or going to bed, making some food, or going for a walk, bike ride, or some other type of movement.

You'll be thinking much more clearly after you take care of yourself in this way.

DAY 159: **SOME DAYS**

 Some days are just blah days. Humdrum. Ho-hum.

Some days are dull and slow. Some days there's not anything new nor anyone to talk to.

Some days your thoughts are fuzzy. Some days you forget how to dream.

That's just how some days go sometimes.

DAY 160: **BLANK WALLS**

 In college, everybody plastered their dorm room walls with posters, but I didn't. The reason I didn't is because I had no idea what I wanted on my walls. It was a time of transition for me, and I wasn't sure who was or who I wanted to be. As strange as it might sound, I wasn't even sure what I liked.

So I left the walls blank. People would always ask, "Why don't you have anything on your walls?" and I would just shrug. Sometimes I even felt a little embarrassed about it. But I didn't know what I wanted, and I knew I didn't want to force it, so I didn't.

One day I came across a photograph of a woman jumping off a huge cliff into a lake under the full moon. I loved it. I bought it. I hung it on the wall. It was just right.

Sometimes the walls of your life are just going to be blank. It's okay. Don't force it. Someday something will appear, and it will be just right.

DAY 161: **FAIL FAST**

 Hurry up and fail. Quick! Do it! Fall flat on your face. Make a spectacular fool of yourself.

It's going to happen sooner or later, so might as well get it over with.

Yeah, it hurts. Yeah, it's embarrassing. But it's okay. Pick yourself up. Dust yourself off. Take a breath. Take a walk. Say a prayer. And notice: You didn't die.

The more you fail, the more you'll see that failure is not a tragedy, but an essential step in learning, growing, and achieving your goals.

Now hurry up and get back at it. Go fail again!

DAY 162: **YOU CANNOT BE A FAILURE**

 You cannot be a failure. It is essential that you know this.

While you will *experience* failure many times in your life, you cannot *be* a failure.

You are not a failure.

You are a miraculous living creature full of spirit and stardust.

Sometimes you will succeed at things you try. Sometimes you will fail at things you try.

Either way, you are still a miraculous living creature full of spirit and stardust.

You are flesh and bones and magic.

You cannot be a failure.

DAY 163: **BE WHO YOU WANT TO BE**

 Who you are and who you want to be can be the exact same thing.

All you must do is choose.

Choose to want to be who you are.

Choose to keep becoming who you want to be.

DAY 164: **HIGHEST SELF**

 Who is your highest self? I know you know her. You might not have the words to easily describe your highest self, but I know that you can feel her.

Mainstream culture does not usually encourage people to act in alignment with their highest selves. All around us, we see greed and superficiality rewarded with fame and money.

You might have forgotten her, but you do have a connection to your highest self. Your highest self speaks quietly through gut instincts, soft whispers, and longings placed inside your heart. She is always accessible to you. You just have to be brave enough to listen.

You can think of your highest self in many ways. She is your soul. She is your inner light, your inner teacher, your inner wisdom. Your highest self is your essential nature. She is God moving through you.

DAY 165: **WRITING WHAT YOU KNOW**

 What is something you know, but were never explicitly told?

What is the earliest thing you remember knowing for sure?

What do you know for sure, without question, to be 100 percent true about yourself?

Who are you at your most ideal? Who are you in your core? Who are you on your best days?

Who are you in the eyes of the person who loves you the most? If you don't know who loves you the most, you can imagine this person and answer from their perspective.

Write freely the answers to these questions along with any others they inspire.

DAY 166: **TO QUOTE MAY SARTON**

 "We have to dare to be ourselves, however frightening or strange that self may prove to be."

These words are from May Sarton, a poet, novelist, and memoirist.

What does May Sarton's quote from above mean to you? Why might it be frightening for a person to be themselves? Do you ever feel this way? Write freely in your journal or on a piece of paper about how you interpret her words.

DAY 167: **BRAVE**

 What is something you really want to do, but feel afraid to do?

To be brave is to be afraid, but to do that thing anyway.

The butterflies in your stomach, the jittery feeling in your feet, the lump in your throat—these are not reasons to turn back. This is what excitement feels like. This is what happens as you step outside your comfort zone, just before you discover something new.

You can be afraid, but you can do it anyway. Courage is a muscle. If you use it, it will grow.

Don't think too hard. Take one step, and then another. Breathe into your belly. Keep feeling your feet on the ground.

Be afraid and do it anyway.

That's what it means to be brave.

DAY 168: **BRAVERY BITES**

 You can practice bravery in itty bitty bites.

You don't have to dive off the deep end. You can dip your toe in.

You don't have to drink the whole gallon. You can take a sip.

You don't have to start up a conversation with somebody new. You can simply look in their direction.

You don't have to perform your song in front of a big crowd. You can perform it to your little sister's teddy bears. And then you can perform it to your favorite uncle. And then, if you want, you can perform for three very kind friends.

Bravery can build slowly, in little steps over time.

DAY 169: A PRACTICE TO CALM YOUR NERVES

 Here's a practice for when you are nervous or overwhelmed, like before you have to give a presentation in class or when you are talking to somebody you have a crush on.

First, feel your feet on the ground. If you are sitting, also feel the weight of your butt in the chair.

Second, notice your breath. You don't have to make your breath big or small. Simply notice that breath is flowing in and out. You are alive.

Third, look around you. Move your eyes and your head if you want to. Notice what you see. List it: A silver clock, a crow, a lady walking a dog, a red backpack.

Repeat steps one through three until you feel a little less nervous or overwhelmed. Do it all day if you need to.

DAY 170: NO SINGLE WAY

There is no one single way to be beautiful. (If someone says there is, they're wrong.)

There is no official definition of true beauty. (If someone tells you they have an app that rates what is beautiful and what isn't, they're confused.)

Beauty is in the eye of the beholder. This means that we each decide for ourselves what is beautiful.

Can you see beauty in yourself?

No?

Look closer. Choose one thing that is beautiful about yourself. This isn't about what you think others might find beautiful. It's about where you find beauty in you.

Still don't see it? Keep looking. It's there.

DAY 171: **RISE ABOVE**

 Help a girl out. Lend a hand. Be a role model. Give your ear.

No need to be catty. No need to compete. There is plenty of room for victorious girls in this world. Opportunities are endless. No need to be jealous.

Jealousy is for small, unimaginative minds. That is not you, dear girl. No. You are far too great for that.

DAY 172: **OF COURSE YOU DO**

 She told her mom, "I feel nervous, and I don't know why."

Her mom replied, "Of course you do, sweetie. You're a tiny human on a big gigantic ball that is floating in space, and you don't know how you got here and you don't know where you're going. We're all nervous on this never-ending cosmic roller coaster."

That made them both laugh.

DAY 173: **NOTICE AN ICE CUBE MELTING**

 Place an ice cube on your hand.

Feel its temperature.

Watch it as it becomes a pool.

Notice how it feels as it changes from solid to liquid.

Think only about the ice cube and its dissolving for those brief few minutes.

Can you stay present to it?

DAY 174: **MINDFULNESS**

 Mindfulness is the skill of living in the present moment, paying close attention to the task at hand. It is the skill of noticing when your mind wanders and gently bringing it back to focus on what you are doing right now.

It seems simple, but it requires practice to live your life in the present. Most of us spend our time toggling between rehashing things from the past and imagining what might happen in the future.

Have you ever been reading or watching a program only to realize that your mind is off somewhere else, like having a fight in your mind with your friend about something that happened three weeks ago or dreaming about what you hope will happen at the party you are attending this weekend?

When you are mindful, you notice that your thoughts have drifted and you bring them back to what you are doing. Mindfulness is not about judging yourself because your thoughts wandered. It's not about trying to train your thoughts to never wander. It's simply about noticing that they have wandered and bringing them back—simple as that.

When you catch your thoughts drifting today, can you softly bring them back?

DAY 175: **MINDFULNESS PRACTICE**

 Here's one of my favorite ways to practice mindfulness.

Sit down or lie down in any position and place that is comfortable.

Start by noticing gravity in the weight of your body. Feel the heaviness of your body on the floor, couch, chair, or bed.

Then notice the movement of your belly, rib cage, chest, and back as you breathe. Can you feel how air flows in and out? (Hint: There's no right or wrong answer.)

Keep your attention softly with your breath. You don't need to change it, although it might change naturally with your attention.

When you notice that your thoughts have drifted to something other than your body and your breath (which they definitely will!), simply draw your attention softly back. Repeat the process every time your mind wanders. Do this for five to twenty minutes, whatever amount of time feels right for you.

The goal is not to get your mind to stop wandering. The goal is simply to notice when it wanders and bring it back to the present.

DAY 176: **MINDFUL BOREDOM**

 Mindfulness is not only a practice to help you relax or handle challenging situations. It can also help make boring tasks less boring.

Try it the next time you have to do a chore that you do not want to do, like folding the laundry or cleaning the bathroom. Give your full attention to the task at hand. Feel your feet on the ground and the movements of your body as you breathe. Notice the sensations in your hands as they work. Observe the colors, sounds, smells, and textures around you. If you find your thoughts wandering, gently bring them back the present. You might find that through the process of mindfulness, the chore even becomes pleasant.

Life will always be full of mundane tasks that you don't want to do, so it's worth exploring ways of making them less grueling.

DAY 177: **MINDFUL HOMEWORK**

 Here's a trick for getting your homework done.

Set a timer for ten to thirty minutes and vow to be mindful while focusing on your homework for your chosen amount of time.

During this time, don't do anything else. Keep unnecessary stimuli like social media, music, and shows turned off.

If you notice your mind drifting, simply bring it back to your homework.

When the timer goes off, give yourself a five to ten minute break in whatever way pleases you.

Set the timer again and repeat the process until your homework is complete.

DAY 178: **BRAKE**

 Hit the brakes.

Take a break.

Take a breath.

Take it slow.

It's okay to take space, to give it space to breathe.

Take your time. There's no rush. You don't have to decide.

Life is not an emergency. Relax your urgency. There is always another opportunity.

When you do not know for sure the answer to the question, when you don't know your decision, when you don't know what action it is you want to take, press pause. Give it time. You don't have to decide right now at this exact very moment. You can wait. Hit the brakes. Take a break. Take it slow. Take a breath until you know.

DAY 179: **WASTED DANCING SHOES**

 I spent the whole party wishing for one specific boy to ask me to dance with him.

I turned down anyone and everyone else who tried to get me to move.

By the end of the evening I had done nothing but stand around with a heavy heart, waiting for a boy who never came by.

This is an incredibly stupid and boring way to spend an evening.

Learn from my mistake, smart girl. Life is too short and you are too young and too beautiful to waste your dancing shoes on somebody who won't dance.

DAY 180: **INTERESTING**

 Everything is interesting if you look at it close enough and for long enough.

Find one thing in nature and look at it until it becomes the most fascinating thing you have ever seen.

Look at it every day for years if you can.

DAY 181: **EASY MISTAKE**

 It can be easy to mistake drama for true love.

It can be easy to mistake the feeling of wanting it so badly for a sign that it is meant to be.

Just because you have never felt this way about somebody before, does not mean that you will not feel this way again about somebody else in the future.

Maybe with somebody else it will be even better, without the drama and constant feeling of unrequited affection.

DAY 182: **SELF-LOVE**

 There is a magic medicine that can heal your hurt feelings, end your sense of self-consciousness, and give you a great deal of happiness.

It exists. It's free. It's available to everyone. It's called self-love.

Self-love is not about being conceited and egotistical. It's not bragging.

Self-love is about accepting yourself as you are. It's appreciating your mind even if you don't get A's. It's being kind to your body even if it isn't the size or shape or color you wish for. It's forgiving your mistakes. It's honoring yourself as the unfolding, growing, one-of-a-kind human being that you are.

DAY 183: **START WITH SELF-LOVE**

 It can be hard to love yourself if you don't *feel* love for yourself.

Self-love can take a long time—a lifetime even—to feel.

But you can start small. If you don't feel it, you can start by *wanting* to feel it. Say to yourself, "I want to love myself."

When you catch yourself thinking mean thoughts about yourself, hit pause. Take a breath. Think to yourself, "I want to love myself." If you can muster it, replace that mean thought with something kind or at least neutral. For example, if the mean thought was, "I'm so ugly," try replacing it with, "I like the color of my eyes" or simply, "My legs let me walk."

With time, neutral statements can become kind ones, and kind statements can bloom into feelings of self-love.

DAY 184: **BELONG**

You belong to the moon and the stars. And they belong to you.

It's true. The elements that make up your body—oxygen, hydrogen, carbon, and more—were made inside a star, and now they are inside of you.

You belong to Mother Earth. Why else would she give you water to drink and air to breathe? You are hers and she wants you to flourish and grow.

You belong to your great, great, great, great, great, great grandmother. Her genes live inside your bones.

You belong to all the dogs and all the cats whose heads you ever kissed and bellies you ever scratched. They love you forever for that.

You belong to the songs that make you dance and to the jokes that make you laugh.

You belong here, under the moon and the stars.

And it all belongs to you.

DAY 185: PRESCRIPTION FOR WHEN YOUR FRIENDS EXCLUDE YOU

 Ouch! That hurts.

First and foremost, don't take it personally. When you find your thoughts wandering toward, "Something's wrong with me," hit *pause*. Replace your thought with, "That's just how people act sometimes." It's true. That's just how people act sometimes.

If you feel comfortable, say something. Tell your friends, "I feel hurt that you didn't invite me." You might learn something about their reasoning that actually makes sense and helps ease your hurt.

Or maybe it's that you are growing apart, or maybe your friends are just mean, in which case: Ouch! That hurts.

Comfort yourself and move along. Let go and open your heart and mind to the possibility of new friends entering your life.

DAY 186: **MEDICINE FOR HARD TIMES**

 Move your body. Walk, run, ride, skip, play a sport.

Listen to music. Dance. Sing along.

Express yourself. Write it out. Draw. Paint. Play an instrument.

Pray to the universe, to a higher power, to the spirit of your grandmother.

Eat something warm and healthy.

Talk to somebody kind. Get advice from somebody wise.

Cry it out. Wash it off. Take a shower. Take a bath. Take a swim. Take a nap.

Touch nature. Put your hands in the dirt. Walk under the trees. Look up into the sky.

Read words that speak to your circumstances. Watch a movie that shifts your perspective.

DAY 187: **UNSOLICITED ADVICE ABOUT TEXTING**

 Save texting for lighthearted and fun exchanges. Do not have important conversations via text.

While it is way easier to communicate via text, it's also kind of a cop-out.

Learning to have emotional conversations face to face with people requires bravery, but it is a skill worth cultivating because it will enhance the quality of your relationships for the rest of your life.

Do not engage in an argument over text. Do not break with somebody over text. Do not try to figure out why your friend is mad at you over text. You can use text to figure out a time to talk, but don't get into any hard conversations until you are face to face.

DAY 188: **UNSOLICITED ADVICE ABOUT SOCIAL MEDIA**

 Use social media to enhance real-life relationships.

Only follow people who have something genuine to teach or offer you.

Social media should leave you feeling connected, inspired, and happier than you were before you logged on.

Unfollow anybody whose posts leave you feeling jealous, competitive, unattractive, untalented, or less than for any reason whatsoever.

If somebody unfollows you, don't sweat it. Don't take it personally. Seriously! Just don't even think about it. There are far more important places for you to focus your attention in your life.

Don't post anything you would be ashamed for your grandmother to see. I know it might be hard to imagine yourself outside your teenage years, but anything you post now can stick around and bite you in the butt later in life.

DAY 189: **UNSOLICITED ADVICE ABOUT HOMEWORK**

 Remember that the hardest part of doing your homework is getting started. Once you begin, you're basically halfway done, because you've already gotten past the biggest hurdle.

Do it right now. Now is better than later.

Find or create a space dedicated to homework. If you always do your homework in the same place, every time you sit down in that place, your brain will kick into knowing that it is time to focus and learn. Preferably this space will not be your bed.

Do a little bit every day instead of waiting until just before it's due. Doing a little bit every day can make even the hardest tasks easy.

Turn off all distractions. You can text again as soon as you are done. I promise there's no emergency on the other end of your phone. It will still be there for you in an hour.

Take a break when you're stuck. Take a walk. Dance it out. Take a shower. Eat something. Then get back to it.

DAY 190: **UNSOLICITED ADVICE ABOUT MONEY**

 Get a job when you can, as soon as you can, even if it's just for a few hours a week.

Learn to read your paycheck. Has some money been taken out for taxes, social security, insurance, or retirement? Do you know where those funds go?

Save 10 percent of everything you earn; put the money into an account that you vow not to touch until you are at least thirty-five.

Make it a habit to buy only what you plan to buy instead of purchasing impulse items.

Create a simple budget by keeping track of what you earn and what you spend your money on.

DAY 191: **UNSOLICITED ADVICE ABOUT YOUR PARENTS**

 Try your best to get along.

If this comes easily for you, you are lucky and that is a blessing.

If this is hard for you, you aren't alone. Relationships between parents and their children can be fraught with all sorts of challenges.

Do the best you can to get along, because, for now, you are in their care. Eventually you will be able to live on your own terms.

Until then, it is in your best interest to do your best to get along.

DAY 192: **UNSOLICITED ADVICE ABOUT SEX (OR ANYTHING ELSE THAT FALLS INTO THE CATEGORY OF PHYSICAL INTIMACY)**

 Sex is not a casual thing. Don't believe anybody who says that it is.

Sex is not a shameful thing. Don't believe anybody who says that it is.

Sex is a sacred thing, and it is best when you treat it as such.

Sex is best when you wait. Wait until you are older. Wait until there is genuine friendship and respect between the two of you, not just lusty attraction. Wait until you are comfortable talking about condoms and birth control and sexually transmitted infections. Wait until you can say penis and vagina and vulva without getting embarrassed. Wait until you know the difference between a vagina and a vulva. Wait until you have at least one adult to consult about it, whether that adult is a counselor, a nurse, an aunt, a friend of your mother, or your mother herself. Wait until you feel absolutely no pressure or rush. Wait until you know for sure, 100 percent without question, that you will not regret it tomorrow.

DAY 193: UNSOLICITED ADVICE ABOUT ALCOHOL

 Take it seriously.

No matter how much you believe that it's not a big deal, it is a big deal, especially for teenagers. There's a reason alcohol is illegal for people under the age of twenty-one. As a teen, your brain is still growing and forming many essential connections. This means that drinking too much can have more serious and long-term effects on your brain than that of an adult, and it can also leave you more vulnerable to making poor decisions that you might regret later.

Just because a lot of teens drink doesn't make it any less of a big deal.

AMANDA FORD

There will be plenty of time to try alcohol as an adult.

In the meantime, take the very best care you can of your body and brain. You are still experiencing so much growth at this time of your life; the more you make healthy choices, the happier you'll be in the long run.

DAY 194: **UNSOLICITED ADVICE ABOUT ILLEGAL AND ILLICIT DRUGS**

 Just say no.

Seriously.

Because, and I repeat: *Your brain is still growing*, and drugs of every kind have serious effects on your development.

Whatever potential fun you might have, it's not worth the very real risks of taking drugs.

DAY 195: **TO QUOTE ADRIENNE RICH**

 "Responsibility to yourself means refusing to let others do your thinking, talking, and naming for you; it means learning to respect and use your own brains and instincts; hence, grappling with hard work."

These words are from Adrienne Rich, a poet and feminist.

What does this quote mean to you? Do you agree with her definition of self-responsibility? Write freely in your journal or on a piece of paper about how you interpret her words.

DAY 196: **ONE WAY TO DEVELOP SELF-ESTEEM**

 Flipping through a magazine, scrolling through social media, or watching a show are no doubt easier than doing your homework, finishing your chores, practicing piano, or working on any other activity that requires you to focus and work.

Pleasure that comes from an easy activity ends nearly the instant the activity itself ends.

On the other hand, devoting yourself to learning a new skill, improving current talents, completing a task, or working on a project creates a satisfaction that continues to grow inside you long after the activity is done.

You will develop self-esteem by doing what needs to be done, engaging your mind and body with new challenges, and working toward and achieving your goals. Immediate gratification and pleasure quickly turn to boredom if they are the only things capturing your interest and taking your time.

DAY 197: **ALL OF LIFE IS PREPARATION**

 Opportunities in life come to those who are prepared. If you are not prepared when the opportunities arrive, those opportunities will not be yours to take.

Preparation is your discipline It is the work you put in day after day, week after week, behind the scenes when nobody is watching.

All of life is preparation. One thing leads to the next, which leads to the next, which leads to the next.

What is it you hope for? Prepare for it as if it is coming, as if it is right up the road, as if you will definitely have it in the future. The future might seem far off, but it is closer than you realize.

The future, bursting with opportunity, will arrive at your doorstep one day. Will you be prepared?

DAY 198: MUSICAL YOU

 What songs are on your most played playlist?

How much is your taste in music influenced by your friends?

What are your earliest memories of music?

How closely do you listen to lyrics? Do you have any song lyrics that are particularly meaningful to you?

DAY 199: WHO + WHAT DON'T YOU WANT TO BE?

 One way to clear about who you want to be is to define who you *don't* want to be.

What are the character traits that you definitely *do not* want to cultivate? Why?

Who are the people that you definitely *do not* want to emulate? Why?

Once you define these things, pay attention to your own behavior. Are you doing things in the very ways you claim you do *not* want to?

Interesting to notice yourself in this way, isn't it?

DAY 200: **POPULAR**

 She wanted to be popular so badly that she lost herself. Everything she did—the people she talked to, the clothes she wore, the things she said—was done in a calculated attempt to get people to like her, to admire her, to invite her to parties.

She worried if she was seen talking to unpopular people, she herself would be unpopular, so she was cold and snobby to anybody whom she thought might prevent her from having the social status she so desperately craved.

She did become popular, but it was fleeting and unfulfilling. Constantly shapeshifting in an attempt to earn power and acceptance left her feeling hollow and strangely lonely, because the truth was that in her heart, she longed to be kind to everybody and she longed to be authentic.

It took her time to stop doing things in an attempt to craft a particular image and gain attention.

It took time for her to learn how to simply be herself, but she did it and it felt much better.

DAY 201: **FITTING IN**

 When you make fitting in your first priority, you lose the freedom to be yourself.

You can no longer be remarkable, original, or unique.

When you make fitting in your first priority, you lose the possibility of standing out.

You'll become bland, mundane, and you'll simply blend in.

DAY 202: **RIGHT**

 At any given moment, some things are going wrong and some things are going right. It is often easier to see what is going wrong, but there is always something going right.

What is going right at this very second for you?

What bits of pleasure can you find? What are you grateful for, no matter how small or seemingly insignificant?

Instead of fighting against what's going wrong, can you shift your attention to what's going right and build on that?

For just one day—or even just one hour—ignore what is going wrong.

Put your blinders on. Focus on what's going right. Build on that.

DAY 203: **ON MASTERY**

 Learn to love consistency and repetition. Learn to see the possibility in the mundane. Show up again and again. Don't assume that just because you've seen it before, you understand it. What is something new you can learn from an old familiar thing?

It takes time to see clearly. It takes time to master a new skill. Stay with it even when it's no longer new and exciting. When you stay the course with what is familiar, breakthroughs and magic happen.

Even if you are really good at something, there is always room for improvement. There is beauty to be found in revisiting the basics, in going back to the beginning. What if you brought fresh eyes and an open mind to the things you think you already know for certain?

DAY 204: **A SIMPLE MAP TO ACHIEVING YOUR DREAMS**

 Begin by walking north on Baby Step Lane.

Put one foot in front of the other slowly and steadily.

Do not feel pressured to make a bold jump across the canyon in hopes that you will arrive at your dreams sooner. Bold jumps are exciting, but they are not necessary for achieving your dreams. Sometimes they are merely distractions.

Keep your head up and your eyes forward.

Feel the fire of your dreams in your belly. Let that fire fuel your journey.

Stay on Baby Step Lane, putting one foot in front of the other, until you arrive at the destination of your dreams. Even if it takes sixty-seven years.

Most people give up far too easily—they stop far too soon. But not you. You will not stop. You will not give up.

DAY 205: **IT'S POSSIBLE**

 It is possible to love yourself and like yourself. To be your own best friend.

It is possible to hold steady and rise above.

It is possible to comfort yourself and soothe yourself and heal your own wounds.

It is possible to live a full and complete life even if your wounds do not heal.

It is possible to feel compassion, kindness, and tenderness toward yourself.

It is possible to love yourself and like yourself. To be your own best friend.

DAY 206: **WHEN HE DIED**

 At home, my stepfather was being ravished by cancer. His skin had turned orange, his body was shriveled, and his belly was swollen to the size of a watermelon with a tumor that could not be stopped. He lived like this for many months.

I didn't tell anybody—not my friends nor my teachers. I struggled to focus in school. I got yelled at multiple times by my track coach for showing up late to practice or skipping it altogether.

My stepfather had been in my life since I was four, and he died when I was fourteen. It was June, very early in the morning. My mom woke me to tell me. All I could do upon hearing the news was roll over and pull the covers over my head.

There will be times when life is heavier than you will have words for. There will be times when you won't know how to reach for help or who to even reach for. There will be times when grief consumes you.

When this happens, sweet girl, have faith that you are supported by spirit, god, the universe, creator, whatever you want to call it.

You are not alone. Even if there is literally nobody for you to talk to, you are still not alone. You have yourself and you have the divine, and together, you will move through.

DAY 207: **GRIEF**

 Grief stops your world. You become suspended. Time seems stuck. It feels like you are moving through molasses.

Grief affects your entire body and the functioning of your brain. It consumes you. You cannot think quickly. You cannot focus. You ache. You can't eat, or you can't stop eating. You can't sleep, or all you can do is sleep.

For the rest of the world, however, everything goes on as usual. It's strange and surreal to feel so out of step with the rest of the world. Grief takes you to an altered dimension.

Grief is a holy experience, if not an easy one. It reminds us of how much we are capable of loving. It reminds us of our vulnerability. It reminds us that life is short and we mustn't take it for granted.

DAY 208: **HOW TO LIVE WITH GRIEF**

 Move slowly. Keep your life as basic as possible. Don't make any major decisions if you don't have to. Sleep as much as you need.

Surround yourself with life. Get a houseplant. Cuddle your pets. Go outside to look at nature. Spend time with people you feel good around.

Turn to your spiritual practices and beliefs.

Cry when you feel the urge to cry. Don't shove your tears down.

Talk to your loved ones who have passed. Tell them that you miss them. Ask for their support from the other side. Some religious traditions believe that people can still hear you for many days after they have died.

AMANDA FORD

Do not feel guilty for anything you might have said or might not have said to the person who has died. You can still make things right in your own heart even after they are gone. Don't beat yourself up. They wouldn't want you to live that way.

Know that the people you love live on in your heart even when they are gone from the earth.

Know that healing is not a straight line. It takes time and has ups and downs.

DAY 209: **CYCLES**

 Life moves in cycles. The moon rises. The sun sets. Oceans roll in and out. Birds fly north and south and back again. Flowers bloom and fade. You wake up and fall asleep.

Day by day life spirals around and around. There is always a beginning. There is always an end. And then there is a new beginning again.

You are connected to the seasons, to the shifting light. When the temperature changes, so do you. You are connected to the weather, to the landscape, to the earth. You are inside the ebb and flow.

Can you feel how the seasons and shifts shape you?

DAY 210: **I SEE YOU, BIRDS**

Write a note to the birds.

Here's mine:

I see you, Birds!
Flying there in the sky as if the wind is
your own personal amusement park, roller
coasters to ride at any time.
Sitting there on that wire as if being together
is the only thing that ever was.
I see you. Do you see me?

DAY 211: **TAKE A COMPLIMENT**

Someone compliments the ceramic bowl you made in art class and you say, "Oh no. I totally messed it up."

A friend says, "I wish I was as good at math as you are," and you respond, "Emma's way better at it than me."

Your sister says, "You look pretty" and you say, "Ugh! My hair is the worst!"

Are you a compliment disputer? Do you dismiss the appreciation others give you?

Receive the good vibes that come your way. Bask in the recognition that people give you. Let yourself be appreciated like the unique, one-of-a-kind masterpiece that you are. 'Cause you are!

No need to be shy or modest. Simply say, "Thank you," and keep those encouraging words with you throughout the day.

DAY 212: **GIVE A COMPLIMENT**

It's hard to be a human, and it's especially hard to be a teen.

AMANDA FORD

A simple way that we can help others feel less down about life is to recognize their talents and efforts by giving them a sincere compliment.

It's a fun practice to open your eyes to the people around you and to notice the good things they are doing. Tell your classmate you appreciate her performance in the school play, her kindness, or her style. If you see somebody you know doing something you think is great, don't be shy to tell them.

Having our talents and efforts recognized by others is one of the best ways that we can begin to see our own creations and the results of our work. Your genuine compliments can have huge impacts on the lives of the people who receive them.

DAY 213: **COMPLIMENTING THE MOST IMPORTANT PERSON**

 Now it's time for you to compliment the most important person in your life: You.

Get out a piece of paper.

Write down twenty sincere compliments from yourself to yourself.

Do it! Don't just put down this book and pretend that you did it. Actually do it. It's important.

Need help getting started? Here are some sentence starters for you to complete:

I like the way I...

I think it was really cool when I...

I admire my...

I am good at...

DAY 214: **SHAPESHIFTING**

 Kelsey pretended that his favorite band was also her favorite band, even though she had never heard of them before. She let her hair grow long, because that's what he said he liked. She signed up for particular classes because she knew those were the ones he would take. She went out of her way to pass his locker. She told all sorts of little lies to make it seem like they had a lot more in common than they actually did.

Kelsey's not alone. Many girls morph their personality in hopes of gaining the attention of their crushes. I admit I did it, too.

Girl! You don't have to shapeshift for love. Besides, let's be real: how long can you keep up the façade?

Instead of wasting your time and changing to fit the picture of what you think your crush will like, put your energy into being more authentically yourself. From there, true connections can bloom.

DAY 215: **THE CURE**

 The cure for everything is a long walk.

Take them often.

DAY 216: **TO QUOTE ANAÏS NIN**

 "We don't see things as they are, we see them as we are."

These words are from Anaïs Nin, a writer who kept extensive journals starting at age eleven until her death at age seventy-three. Many of her journals, which chronicle her personal life and thoughts, were published during her lifetime.

What does Anaïs Nin's quote from above mean to you? How is it possible that we see things not as they are, but as we are? Write freely in your journal or on a piece of paper about how you interpret her words.

DAY 217: **CONTROL**

 Here is an incomplete list of things you cannot control: Who your parents are. Who your siblings are. What your parents do. What your siblings do. What your friends do. The tasks you must complete to make it through school. The culture you were born into. Random accidents. The weather.

Here is an incomplete list of things you can control: Who your friends are. How you respond when your friends or siblings or parents do what they do. Whether or not you choose to complete the tasks needed to make it through school. Whether you are mean to others or kind to others. Your attitude about random accidents and the weather.

As a teenager, there is so much about your life that you are not in charge of. This can be really hard, especially when you have dreams and desires that fall outside the rules and structures of your current circumstances.

But in any situation, there are almost always things you can control. Can you shift your focus to these things? Can you see how sometimes adjusting your attitude, response, or actions can actually have a big impact on the way the world unfolds around you?

Can you see how much power exists inside of you?

DAY 218: **MOODS**

 Here is an incomplete list of things that can affect your mood: The food you eat. Your hormones. How much sleep you did or did not get. The circumstances of your home life. How your friends treat you. Whether or not the person you are dating is kind to you. Your sugar intake. Caffeine. Drugs and alcohol. Whether or not you decided to get your homework done on time. The cleanliness level of your bedroom. Your physical health and how you manage any chronic conditions you live with. How much time you spend in front of a screen. What you spend time looking at on that screen. The state of your neighborhood, country, and world. How much time you spend in nature. Your spiritual perspective. The weather.

Can you think of other things that affect your mood that are not on this list?

Here are some writing prompts. Answer these questions in as many or few words as you'd like. What's your mood today? Do you like the mood you're in? If not, what can you do to help change it?

DAY 219: **NUTRITION MATTERS**

 Your body uses the food you eat as the building blocks for creating new cells, which are constantly being made throughout your entire body. You truly are what you eat.

Your food is also the fuel for all the activities you will do during your day. If you eat well, you will be energized and positive. If you eat poorly, you will feel lethargic, fuzzy-headed, and cranky. Poor nutrition can significantly increase feelings of depression and anxiety.

What does it mean to eat poorly? The main culprits that negatively affect your mood and health are sugary things like soda, sports drinks, candy, cookies, cakes, ice cream, and other desserts.

Becoming aware of how often you consume sugary items can go a long way to helping you improve your nutrition and feel better. Ideally, you would consume no more than one sweet treat a day— yep, just one serving of cookies or one soda, for example. Would this be a hard thing for you to do?

DAY 220: **NUTRITION DOS + DON'TS**

 Do enjoy your food. Notice the flavor and textures. Can you take pleasure in your meals?

Don't obsess. There is not one perfect way to eat. There are many ways to fuel your body and mind so that you feel and look your best. Choose foods that satisfy you.

Do chew. Digestion begins in your mouth, so when you "inhale" your food, you are likely to miss some of the nutritious benefits of your food. Can you try to chew each bite twenty times?

Don't go too fast. Put down your fork between bites. Breathe between bites.

Do notice the impact. How do certain foods make you feel in the moments and hours after eating them? Do you notice a crash later in the day after eating a whole pizza? Do you feel particularly nourished after a big bowl of soup full of meat and veggies?

Don't diet.

DAY 221: **MOVEMENT MATTERS**

 I've said it before, but it's important enough that I'm going to say it again: move your body every day in a way that feels good to you.

Movement is good for your body, no matter what kind it is. Movement can help chase the blues away, it can boost your self-esteem, it can help you think things through more clearly, it can help you sleep better, it can help your body become and remain healthy, and it can just be really fun.

You don't have to play sports (although you certainly can). You don't have to sweat (although you certainly can). You don't even have to do it for long periods of time.

Just get moving in any way that feels good for you: Dance in your bedroom. Shake your arms and legs. Take a walk. Roller skate. Climb a tree. Pull the weeds. Bounce a ball. Swim. Jump. Skip. Run.

DAY 222: **DIET CULTURE**

 Diet culture consists of all the messages that tell you that something is wrong with your body.

Healthy and happy bodies come in all shapes. It is possible to be fat and healthy just as much as it is possible to be thin and healthy. It is also just as possible to be thin and unhealthy as it is to be fat and unhealthy. It can go all ways.

Dieting is the act of limiting what and when you eat in hopes of losing weight. There's nothing wrong with losing weight if you truly need to and you do it in a healthy way, but the only healthy way is to establish sustainable eating habits that you stick to consistently over years. Healthy weight loss happens slowly, and truly healthy nutrition does not limit the types of food you eat. Less nutritious foods can still be eaten in moderation.

Dieting itself is unhealthy.

Your health and happiness will not be dictated by the shape of your body unless you let it. Your health and happiness will be dictated by the actions and thoughts that you choose in service of your own best interest.

DAY 223: **WRITING WORTH**

 Girls and women are taught so early in life that the most important thing about us is our physical appearance and whether or not we fit neatly into an arbitrary and ever-changing cultural ideal. We are reduced to our parts, viewed as objects, and judged upon our prettiness. Our prettiness is projected as synonymous with our worth.

My hope is that you will not confine yourself to this appearance prison. My hope is that you break free from these messages. My hope is that you take pleasure in eating, pleasure in moving your body, and pleasure in adorning your body on your own terms. My hope is that you will care for your body out of love, not punish it out of disdain.

Write a list of all things that are more important about girls than their physical appearance. What matters most? What skills and talents do girls possess that the world needs? Write freely anything else that comes to your mind about this topic.

DAY 224: **SLEEP MATTERS**

 The quality and amount of sleep you get will greatly impact your emotions, energy, and intellect.

It is during sleep that your body repairs itself and that your brain integrates the new things it learned during the day. In essence, it is during sleep where your true athletic and intellectual gains are made.

Much of our modern life is not set up to honor the natural sleep cycle of teens. Your natural rhythm is likely to make you want to stay up later and sleep in longer than your parents or your younger siblings.

Unfortunately, this means that you're going to have to be disciplined, which might not be fun, but the rewards of consistent sleep will be worth it.

Here's the main thing: Get into bed nine hours before you have to wake up in the morning. Turn off all technology. Turn off bright lights. Do not text while in bed. (Whatever you have to say now will still be relevant in the morning, and if it's not, you'll be glad you slept on it and didn't write it after all.)

DAY 225: **HOW TO CREATE A BEDTIME RITUAL**

Stop eating food two hours before bed.

Get off technology at least one hour before bed.

In the hour before bed, do things that soothe and calm you. Listen to relaxing music, take a bath, write in your journal, read a paper book, stretch, meditate, pray. If you do these things regularly before bed, your body will get used to the routine and start producing all the right hormones to help you fall asleep.

Keep in mind that caffeine can wreak havoc on your ability to sleep well, even if you stop drinking it hours before bed. If you drink a lot of caffeine (including energy drinks, soda, coffee, and some teas) and have trouble sleeping, you might want to try cutting back and limiting your caffeine intake to the morning.

DAY 226: **WRITING DREAMS**

 Have you ever had a recurring dream? What was it about? Write about the dream with as much detail as you can remember. When was the last time you had this dream? Do you think this dream had any meaning or significance for you?

Are there specific places or themes that come up in your dreams regularly?

Have you ever had a dream only to have it come true the following day, the following week, or the following year?

Write freely on your answers to these questions as well as anything else that comes to mind.

DAY 227: **NO COMPARISON**

 Selena gets better grades than you. Anna has more online followers. Fatima gets more attention for being beautiful. Nina is funnier.

Is comparing yourself to other girls as natural to you as breathing, an automatic response that you do without even thinking? Do you size them up and rank yourself against them? Do you think things like, "I am better than this girl, but worse than that girl?"

The conclusions that you come to through your comparisons might *seem* like factual, objective truth. While you certainly can say that the girl who wins the chess match is better at chess (at least for that day), it is impossible to compare an entire human person to another.

When you judge yourself and others, you reduce and diminish the living complexity of what it means to be human. Can you learn to look at the wholeness of yourself and others instead? Can you see the big picture? Can you see things in terms of variety instead of hicrarchy?

DAY 228: **LIFE FORCE**

 Life force is the energy that explodes a sprout up through the ground, forms the stem and the leaves, and creates a bud that eventually bursts into a flower.

Life force is the energy that encourages a juvenile bird to let go of the branch and take its first flight.

Life force flows through you, too. You are the only *you* that has ever and will ever exist.

Because you are the only you, the way life flows through you is unique. You have a unique expression, and if you try to change it to match that girl over there or attempt to block it entirely, that unique expression will be lost forever. The world will never get the gift of the true you.

AMANDA FORD

Can you sense your unique life force? Can you allow your unique expression?

DAY 229: **PARENT TYPES**

 Some people have parents who are kind. Some people have parents who seem kind on the surface, but who are mean in small ways underneath. Some people have parents who are overtly and obviously cruel.

It is deeply unfair that we cannot all have perfectly loving parents. As a teenager, it can be hard to see your parents clearly.

Here's what you can know for sure: Your parents will make mistakes. Some will be small mistakes; some will be huge mistakes. None of their mistakes or any of their bad behavior is your fault.

This might be hard for you to understand right now, but I'm telling you in hopes that you might remember it in just the right moment when you really need to hear it: What your parents do or do not do is not a reflection of you.

DAY 230: **OKAY**

 Everything is going to be okay.

And if, for some reason, it ends up not being okay, you'll figure it out anyway.

You're smart enough and strong enough, and you've got what it takes to handle the challenges that life brings your way.

And because of that, everything is going to be okay.

DAY 231: **JUDGMENT**

 You get a bad grade on a paper and immediately complain to your friends about how "unfair" your teacher is. Or maybe instead you turn inside and berate yourself for being "so stupid."

When things in life don't go our way, it is easy to judge the other people involved or ourselves. We attach labels and reduce complex situations to simplistic events with "good" and "bad" players.

We tend to think of our judgments as fact, but really, they are not. And while sometimes life is as simple as good and bad, usually it isn't.

When you automatically judge and put people and circumstances into tidy categories, you miss out on an opportunity to gather valuable information that can actually help move you forward toward your goals.

For example, if you look more closely at your poor grade, you might see that you need more help to understand the material or that you simply blew off your work until the last minute. Both of these scenarios are more truthful and more complex than simply labeling your teacher as unfair or yourself as stupid.

Can you notice your judgments today?

DAY 232: **NON-JUDGMENT**

Non-judgment is the practice of learning to state the facts of the situation and your feelings about these facts instead of sticking to simplistic labels.

AMANDA FORD

In the example I gave in the previous entry about your poor grade on a paper, a nonjudgmental way of describing the situation would be something like, "I feel angry that my teacher gave me that grade, because I did work really hard on the paper and I think I deserve a better score."

Can you see how this is different simply calling your teacher "unfair" or yourself "stupid?" Can you see how this explanation gives you information that you can act upon?

You can always use your voice to advocate for yourself. In this example, you can go to your teacher and say, "I feel angry, because I worked hard on my paper and I think I deserve a better grade."

You can't control how somebody responds when you advocate for yourself, but at least by getting beyond your initial judgments you were able to find words for a dialogue. Labels keep situations frozen, while dialogue opens up the possibility of movement.

DAY 233: **UNCOVERING JUDGMENT**

Judgments tend to be a quick and incomplete way of trying to express emotion. If you dig beneath the surface of your initial judgments, you will find out more about what is really going on inside of you.

Sometimes it can be hard to know when you are being judgmental, because so much of the world around us operates and communicates in judgmental terms. If you find yourself feeling emotional agitation such as bitterness, anger, or hurt for no particular reason, it might be a clue that you are judging yourself or somebody else.

When you catch yourself in judgment, ask, "What's under the surface here? What are the facts of the situation? What are my feelings about these facts?"

Writing freely about the answers to these questions can also be a very helpful tool to uncover the emotions underneath your judgments.

DAY 234: **A NOTE ABOUT NON-JUDGMENT**

 Being nonjudgmental is about digging deeper into your own emotional life. It is not about condoning or ignoring truly bad or mean behavior in yourself or others.

There are moral rights and wrongs. Being nonjudgmental does not mean allowing cruel actions to go unchecked.

We can cultivate a nonjudgmental mindset while still holding ourselves and others accountable to high standards of kindness, compassion, honesty, and integrity.

DAY 235: **WHAT HELPS**

 It does not help yourself or anyone else to focus on what you do not have.

It does not help yourself or anyone else to focus on what is going wrong.

It does not help yourself or anyone else to focus on all the ways in which you believe that you are not good enough.

What helps is to ask yourself, "What do I have?" Focus on doing your best with all you've got.

What helps is to ask yourself, "What's going right?" Focus on the things that are going well and build upon them.

What helps is to ask yourself, "What inspires me? What are my skills? What do I want to create?" Focus your attention on your talents and desires. Eventually you will feel less worried about how you measure up to others.

DAY 236: **I NEED HELP**

 Do you ever have problems that your friends don't understand or that you can't talk about with your parents? Maybe you're feeling depressed and don't know why. Maybe you're doing poorly in school and don't know how to bring up your grades. Maybe you're in an abusive relationship and don't know how to leave. Maybe you're abusing drugs and don't know how to stop.

There is always somebody who can help you, no matter how big or unsolvable your problems seem.

When you get a broken leg or an ear infection, you go to a doctor. It's just as important to get help with other types of hurts and struggles. Talk to an adult you trust. Google resources and find out what people are trained to help with what you're dealing with.

Asking for help doesn't make you weak. It shows that you care about yourself and want to take action on your own behalf.

DAY 237: **CRUELTY**

 There are people in the world who do cruel things. My greatest hope is that you never have to experience this cruelty firsthand.

If you do find yourself a victim of somebody else's mean or evil behavior, whether from a family member, a teacher, a pastor, a friend, or a stranger on the internet, know that it is not your fault. We can sometimes blame awful situations on ourselves, feeling ashamed and thinking of all the things we could have done differently to prevent it.

Do not be ashamed. Do not blame yourself. Do not stay frozen. Instead, reach out for help.

Seek support as soon as you can, maybe even before you feel ready. Talk to a trusted adult. If you don't have one, ask a kind teacher or a school counselor, or else search the internet for resources in your area.

Although you might feel alone, you are not. I guarantee you that there are people who have experienced the same type of cruelty that you are struggling to comprehend, people who have survived and thrived beyond it. Find these people. Let them guide you through. You are not damaged, and this is not your end.

DAY 238: **WELL LIVED**

 The best revenge is a life well lived.

Don't waste your time scheming to launch a counterattack, doing something mean, or gossiping in hopes of cutting down the people who hurt you.

Instead, ignore them. Look away. Go the other direction. Take the high road.

Use the disappointment, the embarrassment, the heartbreak to make yourself stronger, smarter, quicker, and more beautiful from the inside out.

Ignore the haters. Keep your eyes on your prize.

The best revenge is to live your life to its fullest.

DAY 239: **DON'T BE MAD FOR BEING SAD**

 When Yumi's boyfriend broke up with her, she was shocked and devastated. They had been together for two months, and she adored him.

Her mom told her, "Get over it. He's not worth it. Stop moping around. There's no reason to be so sad."

Yumi tried to stop feeling sad, but the heaviness in her body, the fuzziness in her mind, the sigh in her heart, and the tears in her eyes all persisted.

She berated herself, "Why can't I stop feeling sad? What's wrong with me?"

Poor Yumi. In addition to feeling hurt about her breakup, she was now feeling mad at herself for not getting over it quicker. She piled upset on top of upset.

Can you see how being mad isn't helpful here? See how being mad for feeling sad makes it worse? Why do this to yourself?

DAY 240: **DON'T WASTE YOUR TEARS**

 While it is true that we want to allow ourselves to feel what we feel without shaming or scolding ourselves about our feelings, it is also true that sometimes we waste our time being sad about people who truly are not worth our sadness.

If I had a penny for every mean person that I wasted my time worrying about why they treated me the way they did, I would be a rich woman. But I don't have any pennies from those tears, just a whole lot of time that I can't get back. I know there are a lot of other women who would say the same.

Remember, smart girl, feel what you need to feel, but don't dwell. Sometimes you just have to make up your mind to stop being sad and move on.

DAY 241: **YOUR GREATEST**

 What is your greatest potential?

Take a moment to visualize yourself at your very best. How do you behave? What do you say? How do you move through the world? Actually see yourself in your mind's eye acting in alignment with your greatest potential.

Remind yourself of your greatest potential every day. This is what you are capable of. Do not let anyone convince you otherwise. Do not succumb to peer pressure that pulls you down.

You were born to be the greatest version of yourself. It's up to you to choose it.

DAY 242: **ALWAYS**

 Be who you are.

Trust yourself.

Keep moving.

You've got this.

DAY 243: **GIFTS FROM THE UNIVERSE**

 A college painting professor I had was famous for a line he repeated to us as we worked: "There are no mistakes, only gifts from the universe."

He encouraged us to view bleeding paint, shaky lines, and botched compositions not as failures on our part, but as surprise opportunities given to us in order to create better work.

Mistakes of all kinds give us opportunities to solve new problems and to learn about ourselves and the world. When you think about them this way, each mistake becomes a gift of sorts. In order to claim the gift, all you must do is step back, take a breath, look closely at the circumstances of your situation, and work to turn that mistake into a positive part of the beautiful piece of art that is your life.

DAY 244: **SAFE SEXTING**

 There is no such thing as a safe sext.

There is no such thing as a safe sext.

There is no such thing as a safe sext.

Do you feel me?

DAY 245: **WORK ETHIC**

 Your work ethic is your willingness to put forth your best effort. It is the understanding that completing a task with focus and attention is a reward in itself, regardless of the outcome.

Your work ethic is your self-discipline and your ability to put off fun until after the work is done. Can you stick with a task even when it's challenging, even when you aren't sure how it will turn out?

Can you find satisfaction in a job well done? The most important part of your work ethic is not your final grades and test scores. The most important part of your work ethic is not whether or not you made the team, received the award, or earned the coveted spot.

The most important part about your work ethic is your attitude, your willingness to do your best every time and to allow yourself grace when you fail so that you can learn over time.

Where is your work ethic strong? Where is your work ethic weak?

DAY 246: WHAT IF

 What if you thought of the work you needed to do as if it was a privilege that you got to do it?

What if you saw your homework, chores, and practices as opportunities to strengthen your skills and demonstrate your maturity?

What if you thought of a job well done as an expression of your individuality and character?

What if you found pleasure in your work?

What if you shifted your focus from having fun to finding fulfillment?

Can you see how a sense of accomplishment makes you feel happy and engaged in life, as though the possibilities are plentiful?

AMANDA FORD

DAY 247: **TO QUOTE SIMONE WEIL**

 "Even if our efforts of attention seem for years to be producing no result, one day a light that is in exact proportion to them will flood the soul."

These are the words of Simone Weil, a philosopher, activist, and mystic.

What does Simone's Weil's quote above mean to you? What are our so-called efforts of attention? What does it mean that a light will flood the soul? Write freely in your journal or on a piece of paper about how you interpret her words.

DAY 248: **QUIET SPACE**

 It is important to create quiet space in your life. Quiet space is time in which you aren't doing anything in particular, looking at your phone or a computer screen, reading or attempting to learn something new, or trying to accomplish any particular thing.

"Quiet space" is basically just doing nothing. Maybe it's taking a bath, lying on your bed, staring into space, journaling, or taking a slow walk.

Inside this quiet space, your deepest thoughts can emerge, you can hear the voice of your highest self, your imagination can wander, and you can sense your connection to spirit.

Does the thought of quiet space make you nervous? Are you quick to fill every movement with distraction, conversation, tasks, and activities? If so, you can start in small ways. Practice not checking your phone when you are waiting in a line. Stop looking at all screens one hour before bed. When there is a pause in conversation with your friends, notice if you feel anxious to fill it and see if you can allow the pause to go on for just a moment longer than you typically might.

DAY 249: **KISS ME (NOT)**

 "It's going to happen! It's going to happen!" my friend squealed.

The *it* she was referring to was my first kiss, and while she bubbled with excitement, I squirmed with dread. I wasn't ready but felt pressure to catch up with my friends, who were kissing and making out like mad.

That kiss did happen that night, in front of a movie theater with crowds pushing by and my group of friends looking on and giggling. Although I really liked the guy, the time and place were not right and the whole experience was icky. I left feeling sad as opposed to the giddiness I wanted to feel after such an event.

Whether holding hands, kissing, or going all the way, may you always wait for the circumstances to be completely, totally, perfectly right for you. There is no rush, no timeline you must meet, no need to keep up with the experiences of your friends. Trust your comfort level, dear girl, and never push yourself beyond that point.

DAY 250: **TYPES OF CONNECTION**

 We tend to think about close connections in terms of friends who we can tell everything to and have fun with. We also think about connection in terms of dating, romance, and partnerships. These are certainly types of connection, but they are not the only ways we can have close and meaningful connections to other people.

There will likely be times in your life where you don't feel particularly close to your friends and when you don't have a significant other. During these times, it is important to know that you can still cultivate meaningful connections with others.

Over the next several days, we will explore different types of connections and how to build them.

Until then, complete the following sentences (and add any thoughts that they inspire) by writing in your journal or on a piece of paper:

I feel the most connected to others when...

I feel the most disconnected from others when...

DAY 251: **CONNECTION THROUGH A SHARED PURPOSE**

 It is certainly powerful to have a friend that you can talk to about everything going on in your life, but it is not necessary to have a person like this in order to feel connected to others.

Having a shared purpose is a powerful way to deepen your current friendships and meet new people who will potentially become close friends. The mere act of being together and working toward a shared goal can create meaningful bonds without having to say much about yourself or knowing much about the people you are working with.

Playing a team sport, being a part of a theater production, volunteering for a cause you care about, singing in a choir, meditation and prayer groups, or even simply completing a group project for class can leave you feeling more connected than before you started.

Do you participate in any groups that regularly take action on a shared purpose? Can you think of anything like this that might be enjoyable for you?

DAY 252: **CONNECTION THROUGH ART**

 Have you ever heard a song with lyrics that described exactly how you were feeling? Have you ever read a book and felt like the author was writing about you? Have you ever watched a movie and related to the struggles of the main character? Have you ever looked at a painting and felt moved or inspired?

Art is a unique and essential type of connection because it has the ability to express things we might not have the words for or feelings that we may feel shy about sharing with even our closest friends.

When we create a work of art, we express something inside ourselves. When we share that work of art with somebody and they respond to it, a connection is made. When we see ourselves reflected in a work of art created by somebody else, we feel less alone.

Art helps us understand that it is possible to connect with people we don't even know through our shared expression and recognition of the human experience.

Have you ever felt connected through a work of art?

DAY 253: **CONNECTION THROUGH MENTORS**

 Your peers are likely the mainstays of your social life, but it's worth considering spending some regular time with an older person who is not part of your immediate family. Mentors can be wonderful connection points in your life and offer guidance, encouragement, and support. Mentors can be teachers, counselors, coaches, a boss at your job, an aunt or uncle, a family friend, or any older adult who you know, respect, and trust.

Older people can give you perspective that your peers cannot. Since a mentor is not a part of your family, they can also help you navigate any struggles that might occur in your family life. Mentors can also expose you to new ways of thinking and connect you to new opportunities.

Do you have any adults you see as mentors in your life?

DAY 254: **CONNECTION THROUGH ANIMALS**

 Pets are not people, but there is no question that they offer essential connection and love. The energy of a beloved pet can calm you when you are stressed and lift you when you are sad. You feel less alone just being near them.

It isn't just pets that offer us a feeling of connection. Animals of all sorts can give us perspective, helping us see ourselves as a part of the wider web of life. Whether watching birds fly by or seeing squirrels jump from limb to limb, spotting wildlife can be a playful or profound point of connection.

Simply learning about animals that interest you can inspire a feeling of connection. As you get to know more about their behaviors and roles in the ecosystem, specific animals can begin to symbolize characteristics and strengths that you would like to cultivate in yourself.

What is your favorite animal? Learn three facts about this animal that you didn't already know.

DAY 255: CONNECTION TO THE NATURAL WORLD

 In addition to animals, we can also feel connected to the natural world in general. Our very existence depends upon the well-being of the natural world. We need fresh water, fertile soil, and clean air to survive.

Simply touching your bare skin to the ground or standing beneath a tree can soothe and inspire you. Studies have shown that people who take care of plants feel calmer and more inspired. Plants also form the basis of much of our medicine and food.

Looking out into the sky, the clouds, or the stars can inspire a feeling of awe and wonder. We can imagine ourselves as part of an ever expanding, infinite universe. This gazing has a unique way of putting life into perspective and helping us feel greater connection.

Do you have a way that you connect to nature?

DAY 256: **CONNECTION TO YOUR ANCESTORS**

 Your ancestors are alive inside of you. Your genetic makeup comes from them. Getting to know things about your grandparents, your great grandparents, and even beyond can help you feel connected to a lineage. You are part of a family that goes very, very, very, very far back.

Do you know your oldest living relative? Do you have photographs of people from past generations who are no longer alive? What do you know about these people? Do you feel connected to any of them? Have any of your grandparents or parents passed away? Do you ever feel connected to their spirits even though they are no longer alive?

DAY 257: **CONNECTION TO SPIRIT**

 Different religions and spiritual traditions have different names for the ultimate energy force that is the creator and guardian of all things. God, Spirit, Universe—it doesn't matter what you call it. What matters is that you feel it.

You have the ability to form a spiritual connection in which you understand yourself as a loved, unique, and essential part of something bigger and far more mysterious than your human mind can comprehend.

Your spiritual connection will hold and guide you during times when the world is disappointing, confusing, challenging, and hurtful. Your spiritual connection will help you stay connected to your highest self and strengthen your ability to love yourself and the world around you.

Have you ever had an experience of feeling spiritually connected? Do you have ways that you enhance your spiritual connection in your daily life?

DAY 258: **INFLUENCE**

 The friends you choose matter.

The people you surround yourself with will influence your choices and play a role in shaping the way your life unfolds.

Choose wisely.

DAY 259: **FUN VS. FULFILLMENT**

 What is the difference between fun and fulfillment? Is there a difference?

What fulfills you?

What was the most fun you ever had? Why was it the most fun?

Are there things you do regularly that you think are supposed to be fun, but which leave you unfulfilled in the end?

Write freely your answers to the questions above and any other thoughts that these questions inspire in you.

DAY 260: **SMILE**

 Do you know that research has shown that if you are sad, you can feel better simply by smiling? It's true. The basic act of turning your lips up at their corners can help improve your mood.

While smiling when you are feeling down probably won't solve a complicated life problem or make you feel entirely better, it will help a teeny little bit, and every teeny little bit counts.

Try it sometime.

This is also a good metaphor for life in general. Sometimes what helps more than anything is taking action before you are ready, taking action even if you don't feel like it.

If you find yourself feeling down or stuck, try doing the things you would naturally do if you already felt happy or confident. Simply doing these things will help you feel what you want to feel in the same way that smiling when you are sad can help you feel a little better.

DAY 261: **THE MOMENT**

 It is an amazing realization when you understand without a doubt that you are the ultimate force in your own life. You are the decision maker and can take full responsibility for yourself. You can and you must.

You are the writer, the director, and the main character of your life. You choose how you manage your emotions and what thoughts you let consume your mind. You choose your actions. In every situation, your response is your choice. Will you choose your highest or your lowest? Will you cause more hurt or will you help to heal?

The moment you realize this is the moment that you grow up. The moment you realize this is the moment that you become free.

DAY 262: **HOW TO BE A CREATIVE SOUL**

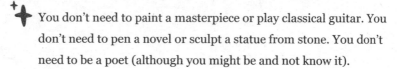

You don't need to paint a masterpiece or play classical guitar. You don't need to pen a novel or sculpt a statue from stone. You don't need to be a poet (although you might be and not know it).

To be a creative soul, all you must do is open your eyes, see surprises, and take delight. Don't be afraid to feel the hard things. Go ahead anyway, keep moving, making all your life your art.

DAY 263: **KEEPING YOUR COOL**

My friend's brother used to tease me constantly. It flustered me, and I would always react to him in a tone of voice that showed how embarrassed I was. This would make him tease me even more. It was a torturous spiral.

He was kind of a jerk, but I loved spending time with my friend. In anticipation of going to her house one day, I made a pact with myself not to react to him.

He started in, and I felt my pulse rise and my skin grow hot. I kept my attention with these sensations and kept breathing. He kept teasing. In my mind, I began labeling my feelings, adding "but I'm okay" after each one. "I feel embarrassed, but I'm okay. I feel mad, but I'm okay. I want to hide, but I'm okay."

I kept my attention with my feelings, sensations, and breath. Instead of reacting in a big way to him, I now rolled my eyes, shook my head slightly, or ignored him entirely. Eventually he stopped teasing me, and I learned a valuable lesson about how to hold myself during challenging situations.

Can you see how this approach might help you at certain times in your life?

DAY 264: **DRAWING RESILIENCE**

 Here's a tool for the next time you find yourself feeling stuck, confused, or sad about life. You'll need a piece of paper and a pen.

Sit for a moment and call to mind your struggle. Sense the feelings in your body.

At the top of the paper write, "What can grow here?"

Now, near the bottom of the page, draw a stem for a flower. It can be ornate or simply a straight line.

Draw leaves on your stem and petals to make a flower. When you're finished with one flower, make another and another.

Keep the question "What can grow here?" in the forefront of your mind. Drawing can help open your mind, allowing you to see new possibilities in the places where you were stuck.

Draw your flowers as fancy or as simple as you'd like. Add roots and birds and anything else that comes to mind. Don't worry about making your drawing look realistic.

When you are done, you will have a page full of flowers, a metaphor for the fact that something can always grow, even inside of struggle. Hopefully this will offer you a sense of relief, no matter how small.

DAY 265: **YOUR CAPACITY**

 You are stronger than you think you are.

You can do more than you think you can.

DAY 266: **A NEUTRAL ATTITUDE**

 There are going to be plenty of times in life when you will have to do things that you don't want to do. In these instances, it might be hard for you to have a good attitude. This makes sense, and it's reasonable not to force yourself to appear overjoyed when you are not.

While you might not be able to have a positive attitude, you can always choose a neutral attitude.

Having a neutral attitude means not complaining, not resisting, and not mulling over in your mind how unhappy you are about having to do the thing you are doing. In short, having a neutral attitude means not having a bad attitude.

You don't have to cheer or even smile, but you also don't have to complain and scowl. A bad attitude makes it worse. A neutral attitude lets you get through it without added drama.

DAY 267: **HORMONES**

 Keeping track of your menstrual cycle is a helpful thing to do on so many levels, including helping you anticipate your moods and energy.

The first day of your menstrual cycle is the first day of your period. Once the heaviest bleeding subsides, many girls and women find that for the first two weeks of their cycles, they have the most energy and experience the best moods. Once ovulation happens (about two weeks after the first day of your cycle), energy levels begin to drop. The last days of the cycle (a few days before your period starts) are the most vulnerable days for feeling particularly tired, edgy, foggy-headed, anxious, or depressed.

The best way for you to know how your menstrual cycle affects you is to track your cycle and take notes about how you feel. You can do this on a calendar, in a journal, or with a period-tracking app.

DAY 268: **YOUR FAVORITE POSSESSION**

 Care for yourself the same way you care for your most valuable possession.

Keep yourself clean.

Be particular about who gets to hold you—preferably only those who are kind and trustworthy.

Have a special place to put yourself for safekeeping.

Never lose yourself.

Because you are irreplaceable—priceless.

DAY 269: **A PEP TALK FOR HARD TIMES**

 I'm sorry to know you are hurting. I know this is painful. I wish I could take away the ache.

Cry if you can. Keep crying and then cry some more. Trust that your tears will not run forever. Let the salty stream wash some of your pain away.

You have the capacity to handle this hard time, you will pull through, step by step. Take a shower. Take a walk. Take a breath. Eat something healthy and hearty. Draw a flower. Write your heart out. Say a prayer.

Is there somebody you can reach out to for help? Do you need help? Or do you just need to be alone?

I wish I could take away your ache. I know this is painful. I'm sorry to know you are hurting.

DAY 270: BUILDING A RELATIONSHIP TAKES TWO

 My parents divorced when I was very young. I saw my father a lot when I was a child, but our time together slowly dwindled as I got older.

When I was fourteen, I hadn't seen my father in two years, but I decided I wanted to build on the relationship we had once shared. I invited him to dinner, but when we met it was incredibly awkward. He felt like a stranger. I had grown so much in two years, and I didn't know how to begin sharing all the different parts of my life with him. To make matters worse, he didn't show much interest in knowing about it.

I went home immediately after dinner and never saw him again. I would have loved to have had a relationship with my father, but he didn't seem to share this desire. I had to accept that his unwillingness to give and receive love was his loss even more than mine. I simply had to move on and look for love from the people who were capable of it.

Not all relationships work out as we hope they will. No matter how much effort you put in or how much you care about someone, you must remember that it takes two to make a relationship meaningful.

AMANDA FORD

DAY 271: **UNLOVING**

 If somebody treats you unlovingly, it is not proof that you are unlovable.

If somebody treats you unlovingly, it is proof that they are not capable of love.

Not everybody is capable of giving and receiving love. You cannot change an unloving person into a loving person. Your love—although powerful in its own way—cannot transform a person into somebody they are not. Only they are capable of changing themselves.

Somebody else's inability to love you has absolutely nothing to do with you.

If you want to give and receive love, you must look for people who are capable of giving and receiving love. These are your people.

DAY 272: **EVERY CELL**

 Imagine the possibility of enjoying yourself, every cell.

Imagine seeing yourself as complete, through and through, every cell.

Imagine there is nothing for you to prove or fix or attain.

Imagine you are complete. You are worth enjoying. Every cell.

DAY 273: **TO QUOTE RUPI KAUR**

 "Loneliness is a sign you are in desperate need of yourself."

These words are from a poem written by Rupi Kaur, a poet and illustrator.

What does this quote mean to you? What does it mean to be in desperate need of yourself? How might you remedy this? Write freely in your journal or on a piece of paper about how you interpret her words.

DAY 274: **BALANCE**

 Earlier in this book we talked about your outer life and your inner life.

There is nothing wrong with wanting to cultivate a rich outer life. Wanting to look your best, to achieve goals, to take care of your possessions, to experience adventure, and to have lots of friends are all worthy pursuits.

The problem comes if you base your entire sense of self on the elements of your outer life, such as your looks, your list of awards, your material belongings, your travels, and who your friends are. Focusing solely on the outside can leave you feeling empty inside when these things fall short of your expectations, which they inevitably will.

The key is to balance your interest in the outer world with curiosity about your inner world. Your inner world is your imagination, your strength of character, your self-respect, your intellect, and your spirituality.

Finish this sentence and write freely about it for a few minutes if you'd like: The most interesting thing happening in my inner world right now is...

AMANDA FORD

DAY 275: **YOUR PATH**

 Your life is not a race, although you might not believe it seeing the way the world around us operates. Everything from the way we learn to the way we move our bodies to the way we engage with our friends has been turned into a competition. No wonder it's so easy to feel like a failure!

In reality, there is no competition. In reality, you are walking alone on your unique life path. There is nobody else on your individual path; therefore, there is nobody for you to race. In the same way that you cannot compare a kiwi to an apple or an apple to a grapefruit, you cannot compare your life to the life of somebody else.

What you can do is to make choices along your path as best you can, step by step, based on the information you have at hand and your own inner wisdom. Not only will focusing on your own individual path help you build a meaningful and satisfying life, it will also ease your feelings of envy and quiet any thoughts that you are somehow in the wrong place at the wrong time.

DAY 276: **THINK**

 We are typically told what to think. In school, you are probably taught a handful of facts about this thing or that thing and encouraged to memorize those facts in order to repeat them back in papers and tests.

You might also feel some level of pressure to think the same exact things that your friends, family, religious community, or culture at large think.

In essence, we are trained to let others think for us as opposed to cultivating an ability to take in a lot of different information and form an opinion of our own.

Learning to think critically is an essential tool in forging a path to your true self.

Today write about the ways you see the world differently from those around you. What different opinion or interpretation do you have from one of your teachers, your closest family member, a friend, and your culture at large? Write freely and quickly several sentences about each of these.

DAY 277: **GUT FEELINGS**

 She met a guy from another school at a party. Although he was easy to talk to and they really hit it off, something deep inside of her told her that he couldn't be trusted.

She ignored this deep down feeling, because, well...she wanted a boyfriend and he was so funny and so cute. Besides, that feeling deep down could have been something else, right?

Long story short, he lied to her on many occasions. It turned out that her initial gut reaction that he couldn't be trusted was correct. In the end, her heart was broken, and she felt foolish for not having listened to her deepest self in the first place.

Have you ever had a gut feeling like this? Have you ever ignored a gut feeling? Have you ever trusted a gut feeling? Have you ever had your gut feelings confirmed as correct?

DAY 278: **FAKE**

 Have you ever been fake?

How did it feel to be fake? Was it a good experience or a bad one?

Are there people in your life who you would describe as fake?

Are there things in your life that you would describe as fake?

Write freely your answers to these questions and any other thoughts they inspire.

DAY 279: **FULL**

 Fill your life with activities and opportunities that expand your worldview.

Do as much as possible, but know that you cannot do it all. Nobody can do it all. To do it all is impossible.

Fill your life full, but don't overflow. Choose only what truly interests you. Dive deeply into those things. You will have to say no to some things in life simply because of time. Nobody has time for everything.

Fill up, girl! But don't burst at the seams. Don't always be rushing from here to there. Choose wisely. Allow yourself down time to stare into space and transition from one thing to the next.

DAY 280: **FAILURE**

 It can be easy to lose faith when you make a mistake or experience a full-blown failure. It can feel scary and painful. You can wonder, "What's the point of making an effort if I end up losing anyway in the end?"

Every successful person has made glorious mistakes, has experienced horrific humiliations, and has lost big time. What makes successful people successful, however, is that they don't stop with the failures. They keep going.

In my own life, I learned to use the embarrassment of my greatest failures as fuel to drive me forward. Some of my biggest motivational pushes in life have come from a desire to prove wrong the people who saw me fail and didn't believe in me.

With just a little shift in mindset, you can turn mistakes, losses, and failures into energy that propels you forward. All you must do is choose to do so.

Next time you find yourself experiencing a loss that gets you down, get out your paper and pen and list all the things you can do to become better because of this experience.

DAY 281: LOOP

 The path from where you are now to where you will eventually be is not paved or clearly marked. Some signs are turned upside down. Some of the lights are burnt out.

In other words: Life is not a straight line.

When I was growing up, my mom took me on road trips to the ocean. Every single time, she'd take a wrong turn and we'd end up driving in the wrong direction.

When she finally realized her mistake, she'd exclaim with delight, "Oh look! We're taking the loop!"

Now, whenever I make a mistake or find myself off course in life, I exclaim, "Oh look! I'm taking the loop."

This is how life goes. You're going to take a lot of loops, so make sure you have your sense of humor and an extra sandwich in your bag.

DAY 282: **YOURS**

 Your body belongs to you.

Your body belongs to you.

Your body belongs to you.

Your body belongs to you.

Your body belongs to you.

Your body belongs to you.

Your body belongs to you.

Your body belongs to you.

DAY 283: **TAKE CARE**

 Taking care of yourself is always worth it.

You can take care of yourself even if you feel bad about yourself or feel bad about your life right now. You don't have to feel good in order to take care of yourself, and sometimes taking care of yourself will help you feel a little bit better.

Taking care of yourself can be as simple as taking a shower and brushing your teeth. It can be cleaning your room, turning off social media so you can get a good night of sleep, or choosing to get your homework done as soon as you can instead of putting it off to the last minute.

Taking care of yourself can mean choosing to do something that makes you happy for no other reason other than that it makes you happy. It can also mean deciding to let go of friends who do not treat you kindly.

What does it mean to you to take care of yourself? Can you do some of those things today?

DAY 284: **A LETTER OF APPRECIATION**

 Write a letter of appreciation from yourself to yourself.

Fill one entire sheet of paper—front and back—with sincere words of admiration.

List your natural talents.

List the things you've worked hard to achieve.

List the ways you've been kind, helpful, grateful, present, successful, and funny.

What are you most proud of?

What do you like the best about yourself?

Write as if you are writing a letter to the person you love most in the world. Leave no glowing word unwritten.

DAY 285: **THERE IS ENOUGH VICTORY FOR US ALL**

 She spent much of her life feeling jealous of her friends. Every small success of theirs felt like a spotlight on her own shortcomings. It was painful to feel as though her friends were not truly her friends, but her competition. She was sad that she never felt truly happy for her friends when good things happened for them.

One day she confided all of this to her aunt, who said, "Focus on your own life. Remember: Success is not a finite resource. It's not like a pizza, where when it's all eaten, there's no more left. There's plenty of room in this world for us all to have victory. Good things happening for your friends does not mean that good things are not also happening for you. Keep your eyes on your own life, focus on what you want to do, and let the magic unfold in its own way and in its own time. And just make up your mind to be genuinely happy for your friends when something good happens for them. You'll feel better if you do that."

And that's what she did.

DAY 286: **THE FUTURE**

 You cannot predict the future. Not even scientists or psychics know for sure exactly how life will unfold. Any ideas are only best guesses and theories.

In your future, things will no doubt go wrong. It's just part of the deal.

But this is also part of the deal: More things will go right.

You cannot see that right now, because you cannot see your future. You cannot see the blessings just around the corner. You cannot see the good things coming your way.

It's true that I cannot predict your future, either, but I do know for sure that as long as you are alive, there is always a new chance, a new opportunity, a blessing just up ahead out of sight.

DAY 287: **TAKE ACTION**

 Have you noticed that it is more rewarding to do something that you have chosen for yourself than it is to do something that you are required to do?

For example, it is more rewarding to clean your bedroom when you decide to than when your parents insist that you do.

If you take action and do the things that need doing sooner rather than later, you will feel a greater sense of accomplishment, earn respect, and likely get some thank-yous from your parents.

If you wait until your parents nag and yell, you will feel resentful toward them and they also won't be as likely to see you as a responsible young adult, which is how you want to be treated.

What can you choose to do today that you know your parents will eventually nag you about otherwise? Take action and see what happens.

DAY 288: **RESPONSIBLE**

You are responsible for all the words that come out of your mouth.

You are responsible for all the actions you take.

Neither bad teachers, bad parents, nor bad friends are an excuse for your words and deeds. Nobody can make you speak or behave in any particular way.

It's up to you. You choose what you say. You choose what you do.

DAY 289: **VALUE STATEMENTS**

 Values can be hard to define when you are growing up and learning new things about life. Even so, thinking about your values can help you achieve the things that are important to you and create a life that feels good to you.

Write a set of value statements by completing the sentence "I value..."

Here's an example: "I value friends who are good listeners and see the good in me. I value friends who are honest and fun to be with." Or "I value caring for and respecting the planet. I value not being wasteful."

What are the character traits and actions you value? Writing them down will help you clarify your own values, and your writings will serve as guidelines that you can return to again and again. You might also discover that there are areas in your life where you aren't living in alignment with the things you say you value. In these instances, you might find that those values are not actually true for you, or you might find that you need to make different choices in your life in order to align more fully with your values.

DAY 290: **TURN YOUR WORDS INTO REALITY**

 It's not always easy to take action on your values. Have you ever decided that you wanted to be less of a gossip, only to find yourself being first in line to spread the next rumor that came around? Have you ever decided that you wanted to get a better grade in history, only to find yourself texting with your friends instead of studying for the upcoming test?

Choose one of your value statements from yesterday and consciously work to live it for the next week. Choose just one, no more. It's too challenging to try to pay attention to more than just one at a time.

What does it mean to live this value? Notice your words and actions. Does holding this value come easy, or do you have to work at it?

DAY 291: **THE GOLDEN RULE**

 Treat others as you want to be treated is the golden rule.

Have you ever really thought about how you want others to treat you? Do you want people to say nasty things about you behind your back, spread rumors about you, or ignore you because they think you're not cool? Do you want people to judge you, make fun of you, lie to you, yell at you, or hurt you?

Probably not. You want to be treated with warmth and kindness. Every person you interact with wants to be treated that way too.

It takes practice to live the golden rule, but you can start practicing right now: you can start with yourself. Treat yourself as you want to be treated and then extend it out to every person you meet.

DAY 292: **WHAT TO DO ABOUT SOMEBODY YOU DON'T LIKE**

 If you don't like somebody, just ignore them.

No need to go around talking trash.

No need to try to convince everybody else to dislike them too.

Focus your attention elsewhere. Look away. Walk away. Block their energy. Keep your mind space available for the things and people that you do like.

Keep it classy. You've got more important things to attend to than being petty about people you don't like.

DAY 293: **THE PRACTICAL BENEFITS OF ATTENTION**

Paying attention is not only a wonderful way to inspire your imagination. Learning to pay attention also keeps you aware of the world around you, and this helps you stay engaged and safe.

Noticing what's happening in your immediate surroundings can keep you safe from physical harm.

Noticing what's happening in the social environment around you—whether in your family, your school, or the wider world—helps you stay engaged and gives you the power to act appropriately on your own behalf. In other words, paying attention lets you be an engaged citizen.

Look up! Open your eyes! See what's going on around you! Keep paying attention!

DAY 294: **SOCIAL MEDIA: FRIEND OR FOE?**

Social media is terrible in so many ways. It exploits our natural human need for belonging and reduces living, flesh and blood people down to mere numbers and statistics. It encourages us to compete, feel jealous and left out, and buy things we don't need and probably don't even want all that much.

On the other hand, social media is remarkable in the way it allows people from across the world to connect and organize. You can find people who share your interests, your purpose, and your vision. Social media can also help enhance your relationships with your friends and family and can be a tool of artistic expression.

Like most things in life, social media isn't all good or all bad. Like most things in life, you have to navigate it using a combination of intelligence, common sense, and gut instinct.

Be smart. Don't engage directly with people you don't actually know, and keep your accounts private.

Be kind to yourself with your consumption. Don't spend hours looking at other people if you end up feeling competitive or bad about yourself in the end.

DAY 295: ONLINE IMAGES

 It can be inspiring to look at images online.

We see the beauty that is possible to create. We get ideas for our personal style and for the lives we want to build for ourselves. These images can give us something to aspire to.

It's important to remember that many images we see have been altered. It's also important to remember that many images we see do not show the entire picture of somebody's life.

Be inspired, but if you start feeling worried or bad about yourself, like you aren't doing enough or you aren't doing it right or you don't look good enough or you don't have enough: *Stop! Put*

down your phone! Go outside for at least three minutes!
Look up into the sky and as far into the distance
as possible!

Breathe, and remember that you are not a cyborg. You are a real person, born to live in the real world.

DAY 296: **THE BIGGEST BULLY**

You sit on the bench more than you'd like during your soccer games. You didn't get a big role in the play. You lost the school election. The person you hoped would ask you to the dance asked somebody else instead. Your friends have more connections on social media than you do.

You think to yourself, "I'm not good enough. Nobody likes me. I am alone." Does this sound familiar?

When life doesn't turn out exactly as you had hoped, it is not a sign that something is wrong with you. There are many factors that influence the outcome of situations in life. Although there might be something for you to learn from the circumstances, your learning does not need to include self-bullying or self-punishment. In fact, thinking mean thoughts to yourself will actually cause more harm than good. We learn better and grow more rapidly with self-compassion.

Don't be your own worst enemy or biggest bully.

Be your loudest, most fervent fan and your most loyal best friend instead.

DAY 297: **ALL THE TIME**

 You cannot be productive all the time.

You will not feel inspired all the time.

You will not be witty or peppy or on your A game all the time.

You need time off, away from screens, away from homework, away from trying to make something beautiful or smart or new.

You need time without effort, time to let your mind be blank, time for your energy to restore.

DAY 298: **SMALL WINS**

 It's important to recognize our achievements in life, stopping to acknowledge our efforts and feel the satisfaction of a job well done.

We naturally celebrate when we reach a big milestone or complete a huge task, but what about all the small wins along the way? If a big dream is reached by baby steps taken day after day and week after week, isn't it worth taking a moment to celebrate the small wins that are moving you in the right direction?

What's a small win you've had today? Can you think of three teeny tiny things that you did well or that made you laugh or that simply felt good?

Recognize the little bits of forward momentum and joy, no matter how unimportant they might seem on the surface. Every bit of positivity and goodness we can notice and create in life is worth celebrating.

DAY 299: **THE METAPHOR**

 How would you describe yourself in metaphor?

Are you the cat's meow, the kitten's purr or the lion's roar?

Are you sunlight dancing across a mountain lake in the morning?

Are you a moonbeam?

Could you be a high-note melody played on piano or a minor chord strummed on a guitar?

Are you the bubble gum pop? The brain freeze of excitement because you ate it so fast? (You certainly are that delicious.)

Are you the eraser on the vintage pencil or the freshly sharpened tip?

Write yourself in metaphor, then put it in a glass bottle and send it out to sea.

Or bury it like treasure in somebody's backyard.

Or keep it in your back pocket so you'll remember forever that you are more complex than the predictable words typically used to describe people—words like nice, cute, smart, and funny. You are so much bigger than those small words could ever express.

DAY 300: **HAVE YOU EVER?**

 Have you ever had a coincidence happen in your life?

Have you ever experienced a miracle or seen something that you would describe as magic?

Have you ever felt guided by spirit? Have you ever had a sign from God?

Have you ever felt the presence of a loved one beside you even though they were no longer alive?

Spend ten minutes freewriting about one or several of these things.

DAY 301: **GENERATIONS**

 Your parents are doing the best they can given what they were taught and what they were given. They are doing what they know how to do.

Maybe your parents are amazing. Or maybe they struggle.

Either way, your job is simple: Do a little bit better than they did. Grow to be a little bit wiser, a little bit kinder, a little bit happier. This is how the world gets better over time.

Take the best of your parents. Improve upon it and become a little bit better.

DAY 302: **THE ONLY WAY OUT IS THROUGH**

Sometimes life is very hard and everything goes wrong and you cannot find your footing.

That's just how it goes from time to time: rough and bumpy, strange and confusing.

The only way to the other side is directly straight through.

The only way through is to feel it all. It hurts! Ouch! The struggle might bruise you, but it will not be your demise.

The depths might be dark, but they are not bottomless.

DAY 303: **SPEAKING HURT**

 She is hurt because her friend didn't show up at her volleyball game like he had promised.

When he texts her a video of a cat on a skateboard the next day, she ignores it.

The next time she sees him, she is distant. He asks if something's wrong, and she says no even though she is actually fuming inside.

Have ever given a friend the cold shoulder? Pretended you weren't hurt even though you were?

I have. Lots of times. It's never gotten me the results I'd hoped for. If anything, it just created more distance and made me feel more alone.

Get your feelings out, girl! You don't have to yell or criticize the other person, but you also don't have to keep them in the dark about how you're feeling. You can simply say it directly, "When you didn't show up at my game like you said you would, I felt sad."

DAY 304: **REAL**

 Your emotions are real, but they are not necessarily the truth.

Your emotions tell you how you feel in a given situation, but how you feel in a given situation does not necessarily tell you anything truthful about that situation.

For example, you might feel dejected and bitter when your friend doesn't say hello when she enters the room. Your feelings don't tell you anything about the truth of the circumstances.

What if you knew that your friend didn't say hi because she just found out that she failed her biology test and she herself is feeling afraid and in shock? That would likely change your feelings.

So remember, your emotions are real, but they are not necessarily the truth.

DAY 305: **GREAT**

 You don't need to wait for anybody else to say you are great in order to believe that you are.

You don't need permission from others to hold your head high, to walk with confidence, to feel your own dignity.

Knowing your own greatness does not mean pushing to be the center of attention. Claiming your own greatness does not mean being arrogant. You don't even need to be accomplished or seen by anybody else in order to be great.

Believing in your own greatness means that you don't sit around waiting for somebody to tell you that you are great. You simply decide for yourself and go about your life, choosing each day to believe that you are, in fact, great.

DAY 306: **CHOOSING YOUR ATTITUDE**

Ellie was complaining to her father about the drama club. "Everyone is so difficult. We spend half of our meetings arguing, and we're way behind on figuring out how we're going to stage the upcoming play. I mostly just feel annoyed all the time when I'm there. I hate it!"

Her father listened intently, and when she was done complaining, he asked casually, "Why don't you quit then?"

That simple question reminded Ellie that she had a choice. Nobody was forcing her to remain in the drama club. She chose to do it, and she could just as easily choose not to stay.

And what she realized was that she did not want to quit. She wanted to stay, and since she was choosing to stay, she could also choose her attitude about the club. Sure, there were struggles, but her complaining about those struggles only made things worse.

You always have a choice in life. Even if you can't change the situation that is bothering you, you can choose your attitude about it.

DAY 307: ASK QUESTIONS, FIND ANSWERS

 Like birds of a feather, questions and answers go together.

Stuck on something? A math problem? A worry? Not sure what step to take next? If you are stuck, it means you have a question to ask. If you are stuck, it means that there is also an answer to be found.

Don't be afraid to ask away. There's no shame in not knowing. Let your questions soar.

Pretending you know when you do not know will keep you stuck. Knowing that you do not know is a step forward.

Asking a question takes you on a journey. When you ask a question, you open the door for discovery.

DAY 308: **WHEN YOU GROW UP**

 Do you feel pressure to know right now what you will do as a career when you grow up?

Do you think you must decide right now what you will study in college or if you will even go to college?

It's okay to be uncertain. Many adults are still trying to figure out what they want to be when they grow up. Many adults make big changes in midlife. Some go back to college well into adulthood.

You do not need to know the answer clearly and with certainty. All you have to do is take steps toward the things that interest you, even if it's just a small interest. You don't need to have a burning passion to pursue something. Simply focus on the things you like and are good at. Do your best with those things.

Baby steps paired with your best effort will lead the way. One step will lead to the next and open a new door for you to step through. Keep moving forward like this. Eventually you will find yourself where you need to be.

DAY 309: **DON'T BE FLAWLESS. BE FRESH.**

 When I was growing up, my mom would often play a song to me that was a duet by a famous musician and his young son. The little boy did not sing on key or hit all the right notes. It was obvious that he hadn't had any musical or voice training, but that did not keep him from singing his heart out.

The song was far from *perfect*, but oh, did it have character! Every time I heard it, I smiled and would have the sweet melody and perky voice in my head for the rest of the day. I can easily call it to mind now.

Why strive to be perfect when you can be real instead? Why strive for flawlessness when you can be fresh instead? Why strive for tight, obvious perfection when you can be free, unexpected, ever-changing, unique you instead?

DAY 310: **MAY YOU**

 May you accept yourself as you are today without comparing yourself to anybody else. You can only be you, and they can only be them.

May you be where you are without criticism that you are not yet where you think you should be.

May you celebrate the wins of today, no matter how small.

May you align your thoughts with gratitude, knowing that your heart will follow close behind.

May you relax into the support of the unseen forces of the universe that are helping you along your way.

May you find ways to let your sense of self-worth be the foundation of every action you take.

DAY 311: **CERTAINTY**

 Have you ever been absolutely certain that something was true, only to find out that was not the case?

Have you ever been absolutely certain that something you had to do was going to be really hard or boring, but it ended up being easy or fun?

Write about these things. Notice when something like this happens in the future.

Can you see how even your own certainty isn't always certain?

DAY 312: **BEHIND THE SCENES**

 Behind every impressive physical feat, behind every exhilarating musical performance, behind every breath-taking work of art, behind every inspiring speech, there are hours upon hours of basic, boring, non-impressive practice.

You can only display exceptional skills once you have built exceptional skills. You build exceptional skills by committing— even just a little bit—day after day, year after year. It might seem boring, but it is behind the scenes where beauty is made. And beauty must be made before it can be displayed.

DAY 313: **CHOICE**

 Life is full of choices. Some you'll make easily while others will be agonizing.

The choices you make are important, because they will dictate how you spend your time and what options will be available to you in the future. One choice leads to the next, which leads to the next, which leads to the next.

This doesn't mean you have to make the right choice all the time (that's not possible!), but it does mean you want to get as good as you can at knowing when a choice is right and when it's wrong for you.

Here are some ways to know that a choice is right for you:

You feel a sense of immediate relief. You feel energized. The choice is aligned with your values. You know in your gut that it's the right choice even if you can't say exactly *why* you know. The choice sets you up for a better outcome in the future (like choosing to turn off your phone to focus on finishing your homework on time so that you don't have extra to do tomorrow).

DAY 314: **IGNORE THE MEANIES**

 Some people are just mean.

If somebody is mean to you, hold your head high. Hold on to your dignity!

The best strategy is to ignore them. Try to remain calm and collected. Keep breathing. Feel your feet on the ground.

If you cry, yell, or get worked up, you will give them the reaction they want.

Walk by without saying a word, or if you are feeling courageous, look them in the eye, smile, and say, "How are you doing today?"

This will show them you are above their cruelty and that their actions cannot affect your happiness.

DAY 315: **TRANSFORMATION**

 May you take your heartbreak, your loneliness, your uncertainty, your worry, your fear and turn it into the most beautiful thing.

You can turn it into art.

You yourself can become the work of art.

We need your works of art.

May you shine your brightest light for the well-being of us all.

DAY 316: **BEAUTY IS**

Beauty is not a contest. There are no winners or losers.

Beauty is not limited to a select few.

Your beauty is for you to see, claim, and express as you see fit.

You can shine forth your beauty into the world, or you can keep it private for only you and a close few to admire.

You do not have to follow somebody else's beauty standards. You do not owe your beauty to anybody.

DAY 317: **LOVE IS**

Love is a state you create inside your own heart.

Love is not about finding an ideal person who makes you happy. Love is not a fairytale like that. Love is not about partnership or romance. Sometimes people get into relationships not because of love, but because they are bored or are afraid of being alone.

Another person can be fun and can bring joy into your life, but another person is not a requirement for love.

Love can be found in other people, but it can also be found in animals, in natural settings such as a forest, and in art. Some people believe that love is the ultimate spiritual truth, the way God communicates, the fundamental state of the universe.

Have you ever had a surge of energy, a wide-open feeling, a sense that everything was right? I know you have had this feeling, even if it lasted for just a very short moment. This feeling is love. If you can begin to notice it, you can grow it.

How and where do you feel love inside yourself today?

DAY 318: **PEOPLE MAGNET**

 If you want to have more people in your life, be genuinely curious about others.

Don't fake being nice or take on the appearance of politeness.

Be sincerely interested.

If you are open, ask the right questions, and listen generously, you will find that everybody, regardless of their age or social status, is fascinating.

DAY 319: **RELATIONSHIP RHYTHM**

 There is a natural rhythm to relationships, whether friendships or romantic or somewhere in between.

You come close. You move apart. You come close. You move apart.

Maybe you've felt this dance before. You and a friend are inseparable for weeks, and then one day they don't respond much. A girl you're into seems really into you too, but then suddenly she turns cold. Or maybe you've been the one to pull away.

This is the dance of relating. Don't let it throw you off your feet. Don't panic, and above all: do not chase after them. We all need space sometimes, and if the relationship has any substance, they will be back.

In the meantime, stay calm and let it flow.

DAY 320: **TRANSITIONS**

 In between here and there is a hard place to be.

One friendship ends, but you have yet to find another. You have moved to a new town, but you have yet to feel at home. You are going to take an important trip, but you have two weeks before you board the plane. A loved one has died, but the world around you goes on like nothing has changed.

Transitions can be hard to navigate. They feel ungrounded and disorienting. One way to help yourself bridge the gap between where you were and where you will be is to focus on the basics. Take basic care of yourself with essential grooming and good food. Take basic care of your environment by cleaning your room. Show up to school on time and get your work done.

Focus on the basic tasks of living, and eventually you will wake up one morning and realize that you have arrived on the other side of your transition.

DAY 321: **CLEANING**

 Cleaning your physical space can be a useful way to clear your head when you feel stuck or down or nervous or cranky.

Instead of sitting around spinning your thoughts while scrolling through a screen, get your hands busy by tidying up.

Organize a drawer. Rearrange your bedroom. Dust the floor under your desk. Scrub the shower.

The mere act of cleaning, adjusting, and ordering your outer world can often have corresponding cleaning, adjusting, and ordering effects on your inner world.

Give it a try. At the very least your space will be a little brighter because of your efforts.

DAY 322: STUCK BETWEEN A ROCK AND A HARD PLACE

During her sophomore year in high school, Sophia and her friend had a crush on the same senior guy. When he asked Sophia to the prom, she was torn. She wanted to go, but if she said yes, her friend would feel angry and jealous. If she said no, her friend's feelings wouldn't be hurt, but she would pass up the chance to go to the prom with a guy she really liked. Either way, she felt like she would lose out.

Life is full of lose-lose decisions. Most choices in life are not black and white, and sometimes you'll have to choose between the lesser of two evils. When you find yourself in a gray area, weigh your options, get advice from people you trust, journal about it, and listen to your gut.

There won't always be a perfect solution and you may be forced to lose something, but sometimes you have to make a choice anyway.

DAY 323: **LOSE**

 When you lose, look at your failure.

Don't merely complain about bad luck or unfair treatment.

Is there something for you to learn? A lesson for next time?

Take what you discover and run with it.

DAY 324: **ALTERED STATES**

 May you find life to be varied enough and vibrant enough that you don't need any chemical substances to help you feel more alive.

May you always reach for the resources and support and care that are right at your fingertips instead of reaching for chemical substances to dull your pain.

The world needs you at your best.

You might not believe it, but it's true that we need you clearheaded.

DAY 325: **TRUSTWORTHY**

 "I told my mom that I didn't sneak out last weekend, and she doesn't believe me," Ellen complained to her friend.

"Why should she believe you? You did sneak out," her friend laughed.

"Yeah, but she doesn't know that because she was away visiting my uncle. I can't believe she doesn't trust me."

If you want to be trusted, be honest with yourself: Are you being trustworthy?

If you want responsibility and freedom, demonstrate through your actions that you are responsible enough to handle the challenges that come alongside that freedom. You have to be honest. You have to do what you say you'll do. You can't tell lies and then get mad when you get caught. Trust is something you must earn and tend to regularly.

DAY 326: **EVERYDAY ROLE MODELS**

Who are your ordinary role models? Who are the people that you know in your real life whom you admire? Who are the people who are kind, whose company you enjoy, who are doing things with their lives that you think are cool?

It can be people you know well or people you know just a little, people in your family or people who you only see from time to time, people who are younger than you or people who are far, far older than you.

Finding role models around you is a way to see all that is possible for yourself. You learn about who you do (and don't) want to be by watching those around you to inspire you and show you the way.

DAY 327: **SO MANY ROLE MODELS**

When I was growing up, it was hard to find examples of potential options for how to live my life. My role models were mostly limited to people in my immediate community and whatever celebrities or famous figures made their way onto my television screen.

You, however, have endless examples of how you can live and what you can create for yourself at the tip of your fingertips.

There are so many paths available to you in life. Pay attention to what people and activities draw you. And then search for even more people doing the things that interest you. Learn about their paths and how they got to where they are.

Looking to those who have achieved what you hope to achieve will give you clues about what steps to take in your own life, and it will open your eyes to even more possibilities.

DAY 328: **POSSIBLE FUTURES**

Write freely about all the possible future lives you can imagine yourself living. Write with as much detail as you'd like about the people, activities, jobs, and locations that are a part of these various futures.

Write about all the things you can imagine yourself doing in five, ten, and twenty years from now.

This exercise is not about trying to imagine one perfect life, but about imaging five, ten, or twenty different possibilities, each with their own unique flavor.

Let your imagination run wild. See yourself in as many different scenarios as possible. The only rule is that each of these scenarios must cast you as being successful and happy with your life.

How many different happy, successful lives can you envision for yourself?

DAY 329: **LABELS**

To be a person is to be forever in process, changing, and growing. You are not a fixed entity or a list of adjectives.

Pretty. Ugly. Stupid. Smart. These are not you, even if you think they are.

These are merely labels.

And labels, like an outfit, can easily be put on and taken off.

DAY 330: **SPACE**

 Give your relationships time and space to grow. Don't force. Don't rush. Don't push.

It can be easy in the beginning of a new relationship—whether friendship or dating—to get overly eager. There's nothing wrong with the excitement and enthusiasm you feel, but it is always worth taking slow steps in the beginning as you get to know a new person.

Have fun and enjoy the process of getting to know someone new, but do pay attention as they reveal themselves to you. You can be selective. The people you let close to you are going to have big impacts on your life. You want those impacts to be as positive as possible.

DAY 331: **WHAT YOU CAN CHANGE**

There are some things about yourself, your life, and the world that you cannot change.

There are some things about yourself, your life, and the world that you can change.

It is up to you to get really good at knowing which is which. You don't want to waste your time banging your head against a wall that will never move. You also don't want to miss seeing the door to new opportunities when you walk by it.

Notice today what is within your power to impact and change and what is outside your control. Where can you take action? What can you let go?

DAY 332: **NONE OF YOUR BUSINESS**

 I remember a friend in high school who was always worrying about what other people thought of her. She constantly asked me, "Does Abby like me? What did Josh say about me?" I told her only the good things that others said about her. I knew she would be devastated if she thought someone didn't like her, so I decided that a little white lie would spare her feelings.

What I learned from the experience has stuck with me until now: What other people think of you is none of your business. People will pretend they like you even if they don't, or they may seem to hate you but are just quiet and self-contained. No matter how hard you try, you will never really know what others truly think, so it's a waste of time to try to find out. Even if you did find out what someone else thinks of you, would it really matter that much? The truth is that your opinion of yourself is the only opinion worth really wanting to know about.

DAY 333: **EXPERIMENT**

 Turn off your phone for a little bit.

Turn off your phone for a little bit.

Turn off your phone for a little bit.

Turn off your phone for a little bit.

Turn off your phone for a little bit. It'll still be there later.

Walk away. Look away. Read something on paper. Stand under a tree. Watch strangers walk by. Talk to your mom.

DAY 334: **ONE CURE FOR LONELINESS**

 When you are lonely, you might wish strongly that somebody would see your loneliness and help you. Sometimes this will happen—a friend will reach out at just the right moment in just the right way, pulling you from your sadness.

More often than not, however, it'll be up to you to pull yourself out of your loneliness.

One way to do this is to reach outside yourself and do something for somebody else. Open your eyes and look around you—see where you can be of assistance. Is there something you can do to help a teacher, your brother, your mom, your grandpa? Do you have an animal you can care for? Can you brush your cat, take your dog for a walk, or clean your guinea pig's cage?

By the time you are done, you might be surprised to notice you feel a little—or a lot—less lonely.

DAY 335: **DISCOVER SOMETHING NEW**

 "You should sign up for a painting class, Astrid," her aunt said casually over breakfast.

Astrid was surprised by the suggestion. She hadn't painted anything since early elementary school. "What? Are you joking? I can't paint!"

"That's why you take a class," her aunt said, "to discover something new."

Her aunt was right. Astrid did discover. She discovered that she loved the feel of the brush dipping into the paint and the gentle glide of her wrist as she decorated the canvas, and the rich colors that filled her eyes all spoke to her heart. She found herself spending hours after school working in the art room. Painting left her feeling relaxed and it was a wonderful way to escape from gossip, homework, sadness, and other stresses of life.

Just because you've never done something before, shouldn't stop you from trying it now. The purpose of trying something new is to try something new. You might be surprised by what you discover.

DAY 336: **REASONS TO DANCE**

Because you did it naturally as a little kid without anybody showing you the moves.

Because all you had to do was hear the music and right away you just knew that it was time to move your little body.

DAY 337: **A CHEAT SHEET FOR COPING WITH HARD EMOTIONS**

1. Name what you feel.
2. Feel the emotion without clinging to a story about the emotion.
3. Keep turning to your resources. Use all your resources. Take care of yourself.

4. Remind yourself that you are not broken. It is normal to feel how you feel.

5. Know that these feelings won't last. Emotions always change. Trust that you will find your way to the other side.

DAY 338: **IN SIXTY-FIVE YEARS FROM NOW**

Here's a trick you can try when you find yourself stressing about something that you cannot get off your mind. Ask yourself, "Will this matter when I'm eighty?"

You will most likely find that most of the time, the answer is a resounding, "No."

Putting things into a big picture perspective of your life can sometimes help you stop sweating the small stuff.

DAY 339: **DON'T EXPLODE FROM BUSY-NESS**

Two tests, a paper due tomorrow, a speech to give at the upcoming assembly, community service, a track meet, baby-sitting on Thursday, and you promised a friend you'd help her study for her Spanish test on Friday: too much to do and not enough time to do it! Sound familiar?

When you break down in tears because you are feeling stressed, when you don't have time to sit down for dinner, or when you can't sleep at night because you are worrying about everything you have to do, you might have spread yourself too thin.

It's okay to admit that you have taken on too much. It's okay to slow down. It's better to actually enjoy the activities you are doing than to constantly worry about what you have to do next.

DAY 340: **MINDFULNESS AT ANY MOMENT**

 Earlier in this book we talked about mindfulness. Here's how you can add it to your life at any moment.

You can use this technique anytime you need help staying present and grounded, like when giving a speech in class, when having a hard conversation with a friend or your parents, when somebody is teasing you, when talking to somebody you have a huge crush on, or when you feel a swell of anxiety or depression.

First, feel the weight of gravity on your body. Notice the parts of you that are making contact with the ground or a chair. Can you feel the heaviness of your bones?

Second, notice the way your breath moves in your belly, ribcage, back and chest. Can you notice how your body rises and falls with your breath?

Third, notice and name your feelings and sensations.

Repeat these three steps as you need to help you stay grounded so that you can do what you need to do without getting overly stressed or upset.

DAY 341: **SAY NO**

Saying no can be hard. You might worry that you will disappoint people. You might be concerned that they will stop liking you.

But if you are saying yes to things that you don't actually want to do, you are hurting yourself.

Today, practice saying no. Whatever the situation is, don't say yes unless it is something you genuinely want to do. There's no need to give an excuse for why you are saying no. You can simply say it.

Learning to say no takes practice and courage, because it means turning another person down in order to put yourself first, but remember: *You* are the most important person for you to put first.

DAY 342: **SAY NO TO ME**

She didn't do her science homework because she spent the whole evening watching sewing tutorials on YouTube. The next morning, she begged her friend to let her copy his assignment before class, but he said no. She was furious, not at herself for slacking off, but at her friend for saying no.

Have you ever been mad at somebody for saying no to you?

Before you fly off the handle, remember that you get to say no and your friends get to say no, too. You've got to learn how to deal with being turned down because it will happen many times in your life.

Let your friends know that it is okay to say no to you. Don't badger a friend who says she doesn't want to go to the party on Saturday night or who won't let you borrow her black sweater.

Show people that you will not pout or get angry, but that you will still be their friend if they turn you down. If you allow others to say no when they need to, they will respect you when you need to do the same.

DAY 343: **GENEROUS LISTENING**

Being a generous listener is about much more than simply hearing what another person says. Generous listening means letting another person talk and giving them your full attention without interrupting them. It means considering the meaning behind and between the words of what someone says. It means listening without planning your response as they talk. It means not simply pretending to listen while you are actually just waiting for your turn to speak.

It's important to have someone in your life who is a generous listener, someone whom you can talk to about your dreams and worries without feeling like you have to fight to get a word in—someone who listens to you without giving you advice on what they would do in your situation.

It's also important to be a generous listener to those who open up and share their lives with you.

DAY 344: **WRONG SOIL**

 A flower in the wrong soil will not bloom.

The next time you start to wonder, *What's wrong with me?* stop and consider.

Probably there's nothing wrong with you.

Probably you're just trying to bloom in the wrong soil.

DAY 345: **LIFE ITSELF**

 If you want to be a leader, to be bold and brazen, to speak up and out, go for it! Follow this calling inside you.

But not everybody has to be a leader to the wide world, be bold and brazen and speak up and out. You can have a small life that fits in the cup of your hands, a life that is quiet and your own.

Your life itself can be your offering. Your life itself can be your art.

DAY 346: **PARADOX**

 A paradox is a statement that seems to contradict itself, but actually expresses a deep and complex truth.

Crying when you are happy is a paradox. Crying is typically something we associate with sadness, so to cry when you are happy seems like a contradiction. In reality, when you cry because you are happy, you are actually feeling something deeper and more complex than either happiness or sadness. You are feeling awestruck, poignant, vulnerable, overwhelmed by love and the fleeting nature of life.

A big part of growing up is learning to live with life's paradoxes. It's learning to be comfortable when things do not fit neatly into a category of black or white, good or evil. Both sides of the coin exist at the same time. So many things are shades of gray.

Can you notice paradoxes around you today?

DAY 347: **OPEN + QUESTIONING**

 Here's a paradox to live by: Be open to everything and don't believe anything.

To be open is to be willing to consider a new idea that is different—or completely opposite—than the ideas you currently hold. It is a willingness to be influenced, shaped, and changed by new information.

Although it serves you to be open to every new idea, this does not mean you blindly accept every new idea as correct. You must think critically.

There are shades of gray in life, but there are also black and white. There are truths and there are lies. There are good choices and bad choices.

Your task is to be flexible and willing to learn new things while also holding strong convictions about right and wrong.

As you might imagine, this is no small feat.

DAY 348: NEW DAY

 Open your eyes. Birds in the sky. Possibility floating by.

Stretch. Reach up to the light.

Vow again to do your best with what you've got. Trust that good things are coming your way.

May kindness flow through you, and creativity, too.

It is a tender thing to meet yourself as you are, to decide to like yourself today as you are, just as you are.

DAY 349: ON FOMO

 You probably think you're missing out on more than you are actually missing out on.

Don't worry, girl. There will be another chance and a better party.

There's always another chance and a better party.

DAY 350: BEING OUTGROWN

 In seventh grade, Lulu and her best friend were inseparable. People called them twins because they looked so alike and spent every moment they could together. Lulu loved her friend more than she had ever loved anyone before. She admired her, trusted her, laughed endlessly with her. She knew they would be friends forever.

And then, seemingly overnight and out of the blue, Lulu's friend stopped asking her to hang out, stopped responding to her texts instantly, stopped sharing much about her life, stopped laughing as much.

Lulu felt like an outsider looking in on the life she'd once had as she watched her friend become better friends with somebody else. Worst of all was that her friend didn't seem to even notice that Lulu wasn't there.

Sometimes your friends will outgrow you before you outgrow them. People change without warning, and their changes are not a reflection of you. Be gentle with yourself during times of breaking friendships. They can be the hardest heartbreaks of all.

There will be a new friend who will be just right for who you are right now.

DAY 351: **MOVE ON**

 Even if you know in your mind that somebody disliking you or not wanting to be your friend has nothing to do with you, it can still hurt your heart.

Human beings are social by nature. We are wired to belong to a group. When somebody doesn't invite you to a party, when a friend stops responding when you reach out, when a classmate is flat-out mean to you, you might feel scared or worried that you are innately flawed and will never belong. It's natural to feel these things.

Don't spend too much time with these painful thoughts. Don't waste your precious life trying to be liked by people who don't like you.

Instead focus on the people who do like you. If you don't know who these people are, look around, extend yourself, be open to new friendships.

Use the power of your imagination to visualize what it would be like to have friends who are kind and loyal. Have faith that these friendships exist, even if you don't have them right now.

DAY 352: WRITING THROUGH TO THE OTHER SIDE

 Here's a writing prompt for the next time you are struggling with overwhelming or painful emotions

Set five minutes on your timer and write freely to complete the sentence, "Right now, I need…"

For example: Right now, I need a hug. Right now, I need a bowl of the soup that my grandma makes, only my grandma isn't alive. Right now, I need a plane ticket. Right now, I need new friends who are better listeners and who don't stab me in the back. Right now, I need a nap."

Write nonstop for five minutes.

If you can't think of anything to complete the sentence, simply write "Right now I need" over and over and over again until something comes to mind.

When you are done, look at your list. Is there anything on that list you can get easily or give to yourself?

DAY 353: **FIVE STEPS TO CHANGING YOUR SELF-TALK**

1. Notice when you are telling yourself something that is unhelpful or downright mean.

2. Choose something new and equally true to say. Instead of saying to yourself, "Your face is ugly," say, "I have eyes that see, and that is amazing" or, "My nose is perfectly shaped."

3. Replace the old talk with the new talk. Every time you catch yourself saying that mean thing, replace it with the new neutral or kind thing.

4. Repeat. Repeat. Repeat!

5. Be patient. Learning to talk nicely to yourself takes a lot of practice over a long time.

DAY 354: **LET YOUR BODY LEAD THE WAY**

When it comes to healthy movement and exercise, your body knows what it needs.

Ask yourself: What feels good to *me*? What do I enjoy? Let your preferences guide you.

Do not ask yourself: What should I force myself to do based on what I see everybody else doing?

Do you enjoy reaching your arms to the sky and twirling your wrists in circles? Yes? Then do that!

Do you enjoy chasing leaves as they fall from trees? Yes? Then do that!

Do you enjoy walking in a swimming pool, picking wildflowers, playing soccer, juggling, or lifting weights really fast while an instructor yells at you for thirty minutes?

Does it feel good to you? Yes? Then do that!

Follow what you enjoy without overthinking, without waiting for the perfect time or the perfect wardrobe to do it. Do it now. Do it for twenty seconds at the bus stop. Do it for five minutes before lunch. Do it for three hours after school.

DAY 355: **IS IT CAN'T OR WON'T?**

 Get clear: Is it that you *can't* do it or is it that you *won't* do it?

There is a difference. Can you see it?

"I can't do my homework," might actually mean that you can't do your homework.

But it might also mean that you *won't* do it, because it's hard and you don't want to make the choice to turn off your phone and you also don't want to stay after class to ask your teacher for help.

Because let's be clear: You *can* do it, even if it's hard. You *can* turn off your phone. You *can* stay after class and ask your teacher for help.

You will lose some of your life if you are forever saying *can't* when what you what you really mean is *won't*.

DAY 356: **TRANSCENDENCE**

 Sadness. Insecurity. Confusion. Overwhelm. I got through these feelings in many ways, but one of the most powerful for me has been to put on music in my bedroom and dance and dance and dance and dance.

I wasn't trying to look good with my moves. I wasn't filming myself to be a social media star.

I danced because it moved the energies of sadness, insecurity, confusion, and overwhelm through me. That's one of the most powerful things that dancing and music can do.

I danced until I felt the heavy feelings lift. I danced until my body was exhausted. Then I sank to the floor, lying there with my limbs spread out like a star, and felt my pulse, felt blood and energy and life coursing through me. I felt my muscles relax. I felt my skin soften. I felt like there was no border between me and the air in my bedroom, no distinction as to where I ended and the cosmos began. I felt as big as the universe. I felt like I was the stars, like they were twinkling inside of me.

This is how I felt after dancing in my bedroom by myself for an hour or two.

DAY 357: **LETTER**

 Write a letter to your four-years-younger self. Get a picture of yourself at that age if it will help you to remember. What wisdom do you have for her now that you've seen what you've seen and know what you know? What encouragement and kind words do you have for her? Write from your heart.

Write a letter to yourself today from your four years older future self. Use your imagination to give yourself advice and encouragement from the wiser version of yourself. What do you imagine that she will know that you do not yet? There's no wrong way to do this exercise, simply allow your creative thinking to wander.

Here's one hint: I am certain (having talked to as many girls and women as I have) that in four years, you will look back on the person you are today and feel a lot of kindness and compassion for her. Keep that in mind as you write.

DAY 358: MAKE THE MOST

 You can make the most of any situation if you find what is meaningful to you in that situation.

Ask yourself, "What is interesting to me here? What grabs my attention? What do I want to know more about? What can I learn? Is there anything surprising happening here?"

You can make the most of any situation if you keep your curiosity at the forefront of your mind.

DAY 359: FIREFLIES

 Launch your pain into the sky. There's enough space for it there.

Throw your pain on the ground. It's strong enough to hold it for you.

Release your pain to the wind, let it blow away.

Send your pain out to sea and watch it sail into the distance.

Toss your pain into a volcano for the lava to burn.

Give it to the birds. They will use it for their nests. Give it to the squirrels. They will stock it up to eat in winter.

Let the rain wash it away. Let the sun dry it up. Let the fireflies use it for fuel.

Aren't fireflies amazing, how they light up in the dark?

You can do that too, you know. You can shine your light even when you feel dark.

DAY 360: **TO QUOTE CORETTA SCOTT KING**

 "No abundance of material goods can compensate for the death of individuality and personal creativity."

These words are from Coretta Scott King, an African American author, activist, civil rights leader, and the wife of Martin Luther King Jr.

What does her quote mean to you? What do you think she means by the "death of individuality and personal creativity"? How do you interpret the idea of personal creativity? Write freely in your journal or on a piece of paper about how you interpret her words.

DAY 361: **BE**

 Be brave enough to speak the truth of what you want for your life.

Be clear enough to see the hard work in front of you to get there.

Be diligent enough to do that work.

Be patient enough to stay the course.

Because sometimes it takes a while to get where you want to be.

DAY 362: **SUGAR AND SPICE**

 You are made of sugar and spice, of fire and ice and everything in between. You are the vast ocean, an avalanche of plentitude.

You are kind, but sometimes you can be mean.

You are happy even when you are sad or sad even when you are happy.

You have hope even when you don't.

Don't fear your range, girl. You're allowed to be all the flavors.

You are the infinite variety.

DAY 363: **PERSONAL MANIFESTO**

 A personal manifesto is a declaration of what you believe is possible for your life. It comes from the word manifest, which means to make clear, to show plainly, to prove. A manifesto articulates clearly and plainly your highest values, intentions, and aspirations.

Writing a personal manifesto can help you focus on your priorities and give you a boost on days when you could use encouragement and a reminder of what you are capable of.

A manifesto is written in short, declarative statements.

I am capable of more than I can ever even imagine. I believe in the power of a good attitude and hard work. I will show my family and friends how much I love them every day. I trust that I can survive hard times. I know that it is the quality of my character that matters more than my physical appearance or material success.

Complete the following sentences to help you get started:

I will...

I am...

I believe...

I know...

I dream...

I see...

I trust...

DAY 364: **WORLD MANIFESTO**

 Yesterday we explored writing a personal manifesto, but you can also write a manifesto for your community. This can be for your family, your group of friends, your school, or even for the entire human species.

It's important to have personal vision and values, but in order for great things to happen in the world, we must also extend ourselves out to take action and engage in community in a way that benefits the greater good.

What is needed in the world around? What do you see is possible? Where could things be made better? How could the group work together toward a shared goal?

Here are some prompts to get you started:

I want to live in a world where...

I believe my family is capable of...

My friends and I will...

This school can create an incredible environment for students by...

DAY 365: **A BLESSING**

 If your heart is open, your heart will be broken, but your heart can fall in love again.

All you can do is do your best with what you've got. That is enough.

May you find something you love to do and may you do it as often as possible. May you find purpose, and may this purpose give your life meaning.

May you choose friends who lift you up. May you know if they do not. May you know when and how to say goodbye.

May you have an older person in your life who loves you and whose wisdom you seek.

May you know your mystery and your magic. May you sense your strength and use your agency to take action.

May you feel your heartbeat and your breath flow.

May you feel your feet on the ground, and may you know: you are a song the universe sings.

Acknowledgments

Thank you to:

My mom for forever believing only the most magical and powerful things about me.

All the girls and women whose faces I held in my mind and heart as I wrote this book: Anita Belle and Sarah. Ella, Lili, Emma, and Reija. Jillian, Ella and Jade. Lucy and Kathryn. Amani and Kimberly. Clara and Vicki. Lolo, Addison, Amanda, and Emily. You were my muses.

My aunt Kathy Jean Bean. My Auntie Jean.

My wonderful friend, Lindy, for your prayers and for always having only good things to say about me. And hello to her spirited girl, Ruby.

All the ladies of the Strong Woman Society for your support, for your stories, for literally feeding me as I was writing, for your consistent and powerful love, and for modeling what I want to be when I grow up.

Brenda and everybody at Mango Publishing for giving this book a second life.

Paul for reminding me to keep it fun and fast.

And of course, my Joe, for forever protecting the creative space, forever protecting my heart.

About the Author

 Amanda Ford is a vibrant writer with a talent for uncovering extraordinary meaning in everyday events. In *Retail Therapy*, Amanda takes an insightful and fun look at the lessons we can glean while participating in a common activity: shopping. Amanda's work has been featured in publications such as *Real Simple*, *Glamour*, *The Chicago Tribune*, and *The Seattle Times*, and she is a regular contributor to the popular travel website Girl's Guide to City Life. You can contact Amanda through her website.

Mango Publishing, established in 2014, publishes an eclectic list of books by diverse authors—both new and established voices—on topics ranging from business, personal growth, women's empowerment, LGBTQ studies, health, and spirituality to history, popular culture, time management, decluttering, lifestyle, mental wellness, aging, and sustainable living. We were recently named 2019 *and* 2020's #1 fastest growing independent publisher by *Publishers Weekly*. Our success is driven by our main goal, which is to publish high quality books that will entertain readers as well as make a positive difference in their lives.

Our readers are our most important resource; we value your input, suggestions, and ideas. We'd love to hear from you—after all, we are publishing books for you!

Please stay in touch with us and follow us at:

Facebook: Mango Publishing
Twitter: @MangoPublishing
Instagram: @MangoPublishing
LinkedIn: Mango Publishing
Pinterest: Mango Publishing
Newsletter: mangopublishinggroup.com/newsletter

Join us on Mango's journey to reinvent publishing, one book at a time.